Enchanted Pedagogies

Doing Arts Thinking: Arts Practice, Research and Education

Series Editor

John Baldacchino (*University of Wisconsin-Madison, USA*)

Editorial Board

Dennis Atkinson (*Goldsmiths College, UK*)
Jeremy Diggle (*independent artist and academic, UK*)
Nadine Kalin (*University North Texas, USA*)
Catarina Sofia Martins (*University of Porto, Portugal*)
Richard Siegesmund (*Northern Illinois University, USA*)

VOLUME 14

The titles published in this series are listed at *brill.com/data*

Enchanted Pedagogies

Archetypes, Magic, and Knowledge

Edited by

Kari Adelaide Razdow

BRILL

LEIDEN | BOSTON

Cover illustration: *Sybil, Dowsing Angel, Merfolk Transport* by Max Razdow, 2019, oil, acrylic on panel, 28 × 18 in.

Illustrations inside the book: © Max Razdow, 2018–2019.

All chapters in this book have undergone peer review.

The Library of Congress Cataloging-in-Publication Data is available online at https://catalog.loc.gov

Typeface for the Latin, Greek, and Cyrillic scripts: "Brill". See and download: brill.com/brill-typeface.

ISSN 2542-9744
ISBN 978-90-04-68148-4 (paperback)
ISBN 978-90-04-68149-1 (hardback)
ISBN 978-90-04-68150-7 (e-book)
DOI 10.1163/9789004681507

Copyright 2024 by Kari Adelaide Razdow. Published by Koninklijke Brill NV, Leiden, The Netherlands. Koninklijke Brill NV incorporates the imprints Brill, Brill Nijhoff, Brill Wageningen Academic, Brill Schöningh, Brill Fink, Brill mentis, Vandenhoeck & Ruprecht, Böhlau and V&R unipress.
Koninklijke Brill NV reserves the right to protect this publication against unauthorized use. Requests for re-use and/or translations must be addressed to Koninklijke Brill NV via brill.com or copyright.com.

This book is printed on acid-free paper and produced in a sustainable manner.

Contents

    Notes on Contributors   VII

1   Introduction: How Do You Come to Know Magic?   3
    Kari Adelaide Razdow

2   Huldufólk   25
    Jesse Bransford

3   Shedding Skins   31
    Vanessa Chakour

4   The Gnome Report from Mother Lode Country   37
    Trinie Dalton

5   Ghosting Ghosts   49
    Lorenzo De Los Angeles

6   Pedagogy of Necromancy: A Workshop Exercise and Its Enactment   57
    Thom Donovan

7   In the Shadow of Toadstools: Fairies and the Natural World   65
    Laura Forsberg

8   Witch Transmissions   73
    Pam Grossman

9   SMART Goals Are Magic   79
    Amy Hale

10   The Goddess   85
    Elizabeth Insogna

11   Reflections on Alchemy   93
    Candice Ivy

12   Shapeshifter   101
    Tiffany Jewell

13 From the Stars or the Booming Labyrinth of the Mind: UFOs, Memories, and Myths   107
    Alessandro Keegan

14 Historical-Ish Fiction on the Legend of Baba Yaga   115
    Jac Lahav

15 The Hag: Metamorphosis   125
    Ruth Lingford

16 Where Is the Lie: Anansi the Trickster, Traveler, NFT-Minter   131
    Maria Pinto

17 Sibyl Pedagogy//Civic Pedagogy   137
    Kris N. Racaniello

18 Traversing the Boundaries of Fairyland   145
    Kari Adelaide Razdow

19 Medusa   167
    Alicia Smith

20 The Golem: On Language and Becoming   173
    Janaka Stucky

21 Hekate: Goddess for the Twenty-First Century   183
    Kay Turner

22 Fool Party   197
    Meg Whiteford

23 Precipitated Spirit Painting and Visionary Space   203
    Erin Yerby

Notes on Contributors

Jesse Bransford
(MFA, 2000, Columbia University) is a New York-based artist whose work is exhibited internationally. He is a clinical professor of art at New York University, where he teaches drawing, interdisciplinary practice, and color theory.

Vanessa Chakour
is an herbalist, rewilding educator, steward of Mount Owen Forest Sanctuary and the author of *Awakening Artemis* (Penguin Life, 2021). Her forthcoming book, *Earthly Bodies: Embracing Our Animal Nature* will be published by Penguin Life in 2024.

Trinie Dalton
is author of seven books, most recently *Destroy Bad Thoughts Not Yourself* (The Pit Gallery, 2018.) She is an assistant professor of Creative Writing at Cal State University East Bay, and lives in California's Sierra Nevada foothills.

Lorenzo De Los Angeles
(BFA, 1995, The New School/Parsons School of Design) His artwork has been exhibited throughout the United States and abroad and has been published in *Psychedelic: Optical and Visual Art since the 1960s* (The MIT Press, 2010) and *Fulgur Press: Praxis* (2020) among others.

Thom Donovan
is an artist, writer, editor, and teacher. All of his writing, including multiple books of poetry and essay can be found at Left Melancholic Patreon. For more information about his art practice, check out thom_donovan_studio at Instagram.

Laura Forsberg
(PhD, 2015, Harvard University) recently held the position of Associate Professor at Rockhurst University. She has published a book and articles on Victorian literature and the history of science, including *Worlds Beyond: Miniatures and Victorian Fiction* (Yale, 2021).

Pam Grossman
is the author of *Waking the Witch: Reflections on Women, Magic, and Power* (Gallery Books, 2019), the co-editor of the WITCHCRAFT volume of The Library of Esoterica series (Taschen, 2021), and the host of *The Witch Wave* podcast.

Amy Hale

(PhD, 1998, UCLA) is an Atlanta based writer, curator and critic. She is the author of *Ithell Colquhoun: Genius of the Fern Loved Gully* (Strange Attractor, 2020) and editor of *Essays on Women in Western Esotericism* (Palgrave, 2022).

Elizabeth Insogna

(MFA, 2018, Brooklyn College) is an artist and CUNY educator. She has participated in exhibitions in the United States, United Kingdom, and Germany with work featured in *Abraxas Journal*, The *Huffington Post* and *The Brooklyn Rail*.

Candice Ivy

(MFA, 2006, School of the Museum of Fine Arts/Tufts University) is a multimedia artist whose works have been shown both nationally and internationally. Ivy is currently a faculty member in the Studio Arts Department at Boston College.

Tiffany Jewell

is a writer and anti-racism educator. She is the author of *This Book Is Anti-Racist* (Frances Lincoln Children's Books, 2020) and *The Antiracist Kid* (HarperCollins, 2022), and she is currently working on multiple book projects for readers of all ages.

Alessandro Keegan

is a painter and lecturer of art history at Borough of Manhattan Community College. He has an MFA in painting from The School of the Art Institute of Chicago and MA in art history from Brooklyn College.

Jac Lahav

is an artist, curator, and children's book author. His work is in museum collections across the United States. Lahav has a BA in psychology from Wesleyan University where he studied the unconscious and witchy things.

Ruth Lingford

(MA in Animation from the Royal College of Art in London) teaches Animation at Harvard University, in the Department of Art, Film, and Visual Studies. She makes short films and has worked on documentaries and music videos.

Maria Pinto

(BA, 2008, Brandeis University) is a Teaching Fellow at GrubStreet. Her fiction has appeared in *Necessary Fiction*, *Frigg*, and elsewhere, and she's at work on a nonfiction book about mushrooms.

NOTES ON CONTRIBUTORS

Kris N. Racaniello
(MPhil, 2021), is a medievalist, artist, and curator. PhD candidate at CUNY, with fellowships at DFK Paris (2023) and Kress Fellowship, Bibliotheca Hertziana, Rome (2023). Racaniello is Co-Director at Field Projects and NY Gallery Manager for Les Enluminures (2016–2022).

Kari Adelaide Razdow
(Ed.D., 2020, Teachers College, Columbia University) curates at The Sphinx. Her writing has appeared in Hyperallergic, BOMB, NYLON, Two Coats of Paint, the Walker Art Center Blog, Eyes towards the Dove, Tupelo Quarterly, and elsewhere.

Max Razdow
(MFA, 2008, New York University) curates at The Sphinx and is an artist and writer. He has taught art practice and theory at New York University and University of Massachusetts, and has shown his drawings and text based works internationally and in the US.

Alicia Smith
is a Xicana artist and activist currently based in Oklahoma. She received her Masters of Fine Arts from the School of Visual Arts in Manhattan, and her Bachelors from the University of Oklahoma.

Janaka Stucky
is an artist, poet, and founding editor of the literary press Black Ocean. His writing has appeared in a variety of publications, and he is the author of four poetry collections, including *Ascend Ascend* (Third Man Books, 2019).

Kay Turner
(PhD, 1990, University of Texas, Austin) is an artist and folklorist, formerly adjunct professor in Performance Studies at NYU. Her books include *Beautiful Necessity: The Art and Meaning of Women's Home Altars* (Thames & Hudson, 1999) and *Transgressive Tales: Queering the Grimms* (Wayne State University Press, 2012).

Meg Whiteford
is an arts writer and editor. She has published in Artforum, The Believer, BOMB, GARAGE, Liber, and X-TRA. She's the author of *The Shapes We Make With Our Bodies* (Plays Inverse, 2015) and *Callbacks* (&NOW Books, 2018). She's the Editor at The Studio Museum in Harlem.

Erin Yerby
is a visual artist and anthropologist (MFA, 2023, Painting and Printmaking, VCU; PhD, 2017, Columbia University). Beyond her dissertation, *Spectral Bodies of Evidence: The Body as Medium in American Spiritualism*, publications include articles/essays, and art writing.

CHAPTER 1

Introduction

How Do You Come to Know Magic?

Kari Adelaide Razdow

Pedagogies surrounding magic tend to be cryptic, with their own cocooned metaphors waiting to hatch. In fantasy literature and the arts, magic ties its practitioners to systems of learning that include traditions, rites of passage, and various conceptions of mastery, while intertwining elements such as transformation, imagination, creativity, and empathy. This collection of essays presents voices from artists and writers who reflect on archetypes and tropes of enchantment in their narrative renderings. Traversing these explorative and fluid realms may at times entail stepping over tide-pools of prior assumptions and surrendering to poetic cross-currents as visions of learning, doing, imagining, and knowing come into focus. In this compendium, each contributor selected a particular archetype to explore and cast light upon the possible implications of pedagogies and magic, while confronting the unknown with both prismatic meaning and prismatic hesitancy. The included meditations on magicians, witches, ghosts, necromancers, fools, fairies, hags, gnomes, shapeshifters, selkies (and so forth), illuminate trails of knowledge acquisition and transmission and raise questions about educational motifs. Threads of enchantment emerge from these essays with highly varied occurrences. No matter the archetypal forms, these stories and vignettes present ways to establish, expand, invent, imagine, and circumvent pedagogies while referencing multi-disciplinary artistic practices. In Meg Whiteford's included essay, "Fool Party," she notes that "Magic can be anything that turns something on its head, a boat on its back, anything which transforms some thing or some idea from one to another [...] This is magic worth learning."

Magic is elusive, yet allows storytellers and artists to experiment with and maintain idiosyncratic, playful, and sincere means of knowledge acquisition and art making, widening the field of pedagogy. The multitudinous discourse surrounding magic and the acquisition of magical knowledge invites both systematic and poetic interpretations, and oftentimes a collision of gravitational fields occurs, with an aftermath that manifests as both a statement and a fantasy. While fantasy is borderless or tends to shapeshift, in this realm there are archetypal images to discern and draw meaning from, as well as depths of folkloric knowledge with trans-historical and cross-cultural contexts that have pedagogical correlations. Engaging with archetypes engenders the possible as well as the engrained. Even if archetypes may be conceived or framed as metaphors for the learning process and topsy-turvy or systematic educational journeys undertaken, they also cast light upon entanglement and the mythopoeic relationship between the unknown and education. While the concept of magic may bind and make more succinct fantasy's presentation of creativity, growth, and modes of teaching and learning, archetypal forms offer intriguing models, conditions, educational processes, and pedagogical aims. How does each archetype reveal distinct principles or heartfelt metaphors of perils, hopes, absurdities, and challenges? Can such pedagogical multiplicities tend to re-codify magic itself?

While locating, imagining, and examining the hallmark attributes of a chosen archetype, each author establishes their own close proximity to or distance from magic. At times, the contributors in this collection draw from their own lived experiences, while applying personal insights through the lens or cloak of a particular archetype. These appointed archetypes help establish frames of thought to creatively interpret or make sense of paths of knowledge acquisition, educational engagements, and trajectories of growth – at times highly personal, and at other times speculative and distanced from selfhood. The contributing authors invoke distinct strategies to chronicle and achieve insight while referencing implicit and explicit pedagogies. Through this tapestry of voices and within the various personal, theoretical, or hybrid approaches, we find articulated and emergent visions for how the fantastic and poetic intertwine in the space of reflexive storytelling. The intersection of praxis and knowledge for each archetype induces a mythopoeic imagination in relation to education, as each reconciles and renews significant transformational elements of pedagogies.

The fantastical archetypes that appear among these pages are named and explicit, rather than presumed or hinted at, even though their existence may simultaneously be perceived as symbolic and metaphorical. While the narrative ratio of real versus imagined scenarios each have their own modulated and poetic sway, some archetypes seem to share the same north star, as they acquire, harness, dispel, manipulate, transmit, and embody magic. In Katharine Briggs' work, *Pale Hecate's Team*, she observes archetypal and folkloric interconnectivity:

> I have been increasingly impressed by the interconnection, though not the identity, of supernatural creatures in folklore, and by the way in which folklore and literature rise and sink into each other. So it is that a

chapter on fairies is full of reference to witches, lost deities, and heroes of romance, that witches creep into demonology, fairy lore, and folk natural history, and that ghosts appear and disappear among the fairies, devils and angels. Without assuming that identity of origin of which many have been convinced, one must admit that the strands of belief are almost inextricably tangled. (1962, p. 222)

While the identities of supernatural creatures or archetypes may be distinct, it seems possible that magic is the glue or mechanism of cohesion, allowing for an entanglement of variable strands of enchantment, no matter the ragtag parade of puckish and earnest actors. Magic and its entwined elements, along with archetypes, have many catchphrases and echoes, and it goes without saying that this collection represents only a shard of all that enchantment encircles – there's no magic lantern to cast light on it all. Furthermore, fantasy contains myriad possible forms referenced and examined in its folds, and as a whole presents a nearly inexhaustible engine for variations of pedagogies.

These essays evoke and reflect on a wide range of arcane characters often arising from myth and folklore, also glimpsed in fantasy literature. Myth and the fantastic at large maintain an endless menagerie of strange and alluring creatures and characters. Emerging from these pluralistic and opaque spaces are certain images or archetypes (such as witches, ghosts, fairies, magicians, etc.), which seem especially familiar. Archetypes, according to Carl Jung, entertain and thrive on the timeless multiplicities derived from myth, while also maintaining an intuitive understanding given their recurring appearance in stories and the present day. These archetypes may become established enough to embody or convey specific educational motifs and models with particular imagined pedagogical aims. The process of engaging with these archetypes presents a lens by which pedagogies and knowledge transmission can be explored.

The forthcoming pages are teeming with nature spirits and phantasms, each with their own associations and pedagogical possibilities and impossibilities. By no means fenced off as evolving conversations, many of these essays have shrouded back stories and herald the illusory and metaphorical devices of enchantment. These many sided vignettes muse on archetypes and the discovery of and process of learning of magic, reclaiming, and hypothesizing enhancements of possible achievements and growth. In fantasy literature in particular, the presence of magic illustrates pedagogical aims and outcomes no matter the means or process of acquisition (which can at times be messy, systematic, intuitive, rigorous, or altogether ephemeral, as magic makes itself known on its own terms).

So how can magic bind the unknown with education, enabling the speculative to supersede the normative and familiar, possibly enhancing notions of creative agency and empowerment? Ideally, at its best, education involves enhanced forms of self-knowledge and transformation. And on its own, magic has associations with not only arcane systems of rites, spells, and supernatural creatures, but likewise involves self-knowledge and transformation. Due to self-knowledge and transformation, perhaps the neighborly admixture of the two – education and magic – may become harmoniously interconnected, while the shackles of the routine are eroded, disrupted, and changed. Often clashing and bleakly unreconciled, magic and education are alternately quite well equipped to enrich and cross-pollinate one another, at times working in concert to establish possibilities.

Within the realm of fantasy, sometimes tenets of magical knowledge are stumbled upon without rhyme or reason, by sheer luck and happenstance, and sometimes enchanted wisdom lies within, as innate or raw talent that requires recognition or cultivation. Other times, magical knowledge and skills are gifted or bestowed by a supernatural creature through some means of transaction, and rarely with no strings attached. Another possibility is that magic is hard won after systematic toil and efforts, requiring resilience, grit, belly flops, and untold failures in order to come into full flower.

Overall, the idea of pedagogies in this book may be framed as broad and open constructs involving ideas of teaching and learning as well as growth. In *Democracy and Education*, John Dewey reflects, "Education is thus a fostering, a nurturing, a cultivating, process. All of these words mean that it implies attention to the conditions of growth" (1916, p. 10). Dewey further reflects that the educational process should encourage and entail growth, and even childlike growth:

> The educational process is one of continual reorganizing, reconstructing, transforming. ... With respect to sympathetic curiosity, unbiased responsiveness, and openness of mind, we may say that an adult should be growing in childlikeness. (1916, p. 50)

Dewey further asserts, "If education is growth, it must progressively realize present possibilities. ... Growing is not something which is completed in odd moments; it is a continuous leading into the future" (1916, p. 56). Trajectories of growth undeniably include plentiful odd moments, as persistent strangeness pops up in life like a proverbial bad penny, over and over. Nonetheless, keeping a hold on possibilities and growth are powerful and affirmative aims, mandating some degree of confidence in the golden tenets of becoming. While

Dewey's scholarship often interfaces with uncertainties, he typically does not touch upon magic (or magical indeterminacy and possibilities), or any of its catchphrases; yet, he does reference the unknown: "All thinking involves a risk. Certainty cannot be guaranteed in advance. The invasion of the unknown is of the nature of an adventure; we cannot be sure in advance" (Dewey, 1916, p. 148).

In *Pedagogy of the Oppressed*, Paulo Freire presents keen thoughts on how education has the potential to activate generative qualities, with an ode to the cultivation of inner worlds and outer worlds alike: "Problem-posing education affirms men and women as beings in the process of becoming – as unfinished, uncompleted beings in and with a likewise unfinished reality" (1970, p. 84). Possibilities also abound in Maxine Greene's scholarship on pedagogy, as she lauds curiosity as a potent and influential ingredient to give rise to strong and cresting inner tides that cultivate our imagination: "The more we can actively and interestedly perceive, you see, the wider becomes the field on which our imaginations can work. It is imagination that enables us to reach beyond, to open up those possibilities" (2001, p. 74). By reaching beyond the known, prying open possibilities, and paying homage to the realms of growth and becoming, the idea of pedagogy is surely not bound or beholden to classroom constructs of teaching and learning. Pedagogies may involve broad commitments, visions, expressions, experiences, imaginings, and engagements of growth which lead to enhanced reflections and transformations. With these humanistic constructs of pedagogies in mind, the metaphoric scope of education includes the acquisition and transmission of magical knowledge as well as more ephemeral zones of reflexivity that include enchantment and self-enchantment.

1   Fantasy and Keyed Up or Keyed Down Worlds

Fantasy relates to the imagination and the imaginary, along with a host of phantoms and hallucinations rather than any singular form. Overall, because of the quality of its inexhaustible constituent parts, its totality remains elusive and changeable. In some cases, fantasy may shed light on truth, meaning, and desire, as these concepts relate to the normal or humdrum of the everyday. Perhaps fantasy is a mirror of reality, revealing difficult truths to grapple with, while enabling enhanced ways of seeing, empathizing, coping, and understanding. In other cases, fantasy may carry us far away from reality, transporting us to curiously scrambled or glittering worlds, towards strangeness and subversive planes, full of pleasure and profundity, or potentially full of terror. The latter deals with being transported, and is less of a mirror than a portal. Portals facilitate multidimensional leaps, providing passage to new worlds, as faraway realms of elsewhere are imagined and crossed. Upon crossing thresholds and being transported, magic lurks, no matter the mechanism of how and why. Perhaps the most riveting fantasy employs both portals and mirrors, inviting leaps of enchantment to encounter other worlds, while amplifying reflections and truths within our own.

To engage with fantasy is to engage with the unreal, to watch for the phantom, to chase the will-o'-the-wisp, and observe the play of the shadow. Fantasy allows us to reach towards and confront the unknown. It occupies an ontological space that enables us to undo the boundaries of reality, carrying us to other orders of experience – other captivating keyed up or keyed down worlds – allowing us to see deeper truths within our own and empathize with the nonhuman and human alike.

Traversing the fantastic is not without impact on reality or dismissive of reality, according to Ursula K. Le Guin. Operating on various levels, fantasy may be commonly associated with the child-like, but even so entails gravity and purpose:

> What is fantasy? On one level, of course, it is a game: a pure pretense with no ulterior motive whatever. It is one child saying to another child, 'Let's be dragons,' and then they're dragons for an hour or two. It is escapism at the most admirable kind – the game played for the game's sake. On another level, it is still a game, but a game played for very high stakes. Seen thus, as art, not spontaneous play, its affinity is not with daydream, but with dream. It is a different approach to reality, an alternative technique for apprehending and coping with existence. It is not antirational but pararational; not realistic, but surrealistic, superrealistic, a heightening of reality. … It employs archetypes, which, Jung warned us, are dangerous things … Fantasy is nearer to poetry, mysticism, and to insanity than naturalistic fiction is. It is a real wilderness, and those who go there should not feel too safe. (2004, p. 145)

Le Guin stresses how instantiating a path through this so-called wilderness may invoke archetypes and the act of doing so extends beyond modes of play and escapism. Engaging with the fantastic involves confronting reality and its tendrils on deep terms; or, perhaps enhances the ability to better cope with reality, without fully succumbing to the fantasist's blow dart. Le Guin reveals associations with fantasy that are not simply whimsical but that fiercely interplay with reality and art. She asserts that by approaching reality through art and archetypes, it's possible to discern poetic and mystical dream affinities, while seeing deeply or coping with reality.

2   Magic and the Quest to Understand Nature

In these essays, we will be compelled to consider the substance of fantasy and magic on their own slippery and elusive terms. One possible way to illuminate the meaning of the term "magic" is to briefly compare fantasy with its less magical sibling, science fiction, as investigated by literary scholar Karl Kroeber. By looking at the two forms side by side, it is possible to see what is particularly unique about each, casting light on the utilities, layers, and meanings of magic. Kroeber illuminates the complex correlations and oppositions of these two forms:

> The genres of science fiction and fantasy overlap and interpenetrate. All literary genres are impure, each partaking of diverse formal modalities, but fantasy and science fiction are especially intertwined because they have a common origin. ... The writer of science fiction extends or projects or draws inferences from what is known and accepted (and the primary known fact of the modern world is that humanity dominates our globe). The science fiction writer extrapolates scientifically, of course, which means that he or she employs the basic style of a scientific discourse – analytical, reportorial exposition: his basic form is scientific reportage. Fantasy responds to the same circumstance of humanity's technological triumph differently, leading some critics to think of fantasy simply as a looking backward. But fantasy, although it may try to recover a lost sense for otherness, turns inward rather than backward. Fantasy is a primary form of literary self-reflexivity. ... Fantasy involves its author in self-enchantment, which leads the fantasist toward a discourse distinct from the realistic, rationalistic, expository forms that undergird science fiction. Fantasy tends toward self-involuting procedures. (1988, pp. 9–10)

While Kroeber maintains that the two genres entertain slippages in many ways, cross-pollinating each other significantly, he acknowledges implicit differences. Science fiction, he claims, is a literature born of scientific processes allowing for analytic scientific extrapolations. Fantasy, on the other hand, is a discourse of "self-involuting" processes; it involves turning inward and self-enchantment. Kroeber suggests that science fiction casts science and scientific extrapolations into the future, projecting certain concrete outcomes. In comparison with fantasy, it is stricter in its treatment of consequence and cause/effect relations.

If the primary substance of science fiction is science (a rational examination of the world), then the primary substance of fantasy is magic, which is, in many senses, a para-rational examination of the world. To some, perhaps magic may be unpacked as stirring enactments and visions towards influencing elements and external realities: amplifying and harnessing mysterious forces that are presumably beyond control and comprehension. Whether framed as an idea, realm, force, practice, power of imagination, or metaphor, magic resists being neatly compartmentalized. At times, through acts of accord towards desired changes and outcomes, a nod to the tenets of magic includes turning inward, cultivating interiority, and interfacing with the natural and outer world in a heightened and cogent manner, while seeing with unbound imagination. These creative acts and visions amplify agency and help establish possibilities, vast and small. Perhaps magic encourages one to see deeply with the aim of reaching a new destination. Perhaps magic aids with the process of conceiving and pursuing potential trajectories of growth and transformation: to second guess how things are or seem to be, to recognize and name invisible barriers, and work towards enacting change.

In *A General Theory of Magic*, the anthropologist Marcel Mauss investigates how the history of magic is in fact linked to science in terms of the tandem quest to understand nature:

> Magic is linked to science in the same way as it is linked to technology. It is not only a practical art, it is also a storehouse of ideas. It attaches great importance to knowledge – one of its mainsprings. In fact, we have seen over and over again how, as far as magic is concerned, knowledge is power. ... Magic ... is concerned with understanding nature. It quickly set up a kind of index of plants, metals, phenomena, beings and life in general, and became an early store of information for the astronomical, physical, and natural sciences. (1972, pp. 176–177)

The alignment of magic with the quest for knowledge and the objective of arriving at deep comprehension are precisely what leads to rich pedagogical implications. As Mauss points out, the mainspring of magic is knowledge, and magic is a multi-faceted pedagogical conduit to further knowledge of the natural world. Magic is also a lexicon; a storehouse of information. Mauss asserts that magicians attempted to systematize knowledge in so-called "magician colleges." We see this actual historical tenet fictionalized in fantasy literature:

> Magicians have sometimes even attempted to systematize their knowledge and, by so doing, derive principles. When such theories are elaborated in magician colleges, it is done by rational and individual

procedures. In their doctrinal studies magicians tried to discard as many mystical elements as they could, and thus it was that magic took on the character of a genuine science. (1972, p. 177)

This systematization of a magician's knowledge stripped it of mysticism and flexibility, as principles became established at the expense of enchantment, blow by blow. Magic was kneecapped by rationality but not altogether nullified. Mauss reflects on the manner in which a magical practitioner's reservoir of knowledge and cultivation of and magic may arrive in many forms:

> The magician is a person who, through his gifts, his experience or through revelation, understands nature and natures; his practice depends on this knowledge. It is here that magic most approximates science. From this point of view, magic can be very knowledgeable even if it is not truly scientific. A good deal of knowledge we have mentioned here has been acquired and verified through experiment. ... The laws of magic ... are really a kind of magical philosophy. They were a series of empty, hollow forms bringing in laws of causality which were always poorly formulated. (1972, p. 94)

Mauss suggests that the nuanced and idiosyncratic conventions of magic align with a "magical philosophy": it is lexical, conversant, and not bound to the empiric. He details the practice of the magician through gifts, experience and/ or revelation, honoring the knowledge they acquire, no matter how scrappy or nonsensical the underlying laws of causality. The acquisition and transmission of magic entertains a broad metaphorical space of pedagogy, encouraging selfhood that cultivates knowledge that interfaces with poetry, music, the written word, the visionary and the arts at large, and beyond.

3   Recaptured Magic and Self-Reflexivity

Fantasy depends on magic, oftentimes unwieldy and in limbo, and frequently these enchanted forces are transmitted from hidden sources of lore with archaic and deep connections to the past. Mauss reveals that the practices and studies of magic have changed drastically over time. In this evolution, collective aims eroded and diminished. In fantasy literature, poetry, and art, a desire for a reclamation of magical principles may be discerned that stand tall with an idiosyncratic yet empowered praxis. Magic embraces otherness, and seeks a reunification with more distant or lost forms of enchantment and its pedagogies. This vital act of recovery is imagined in Terry Pratchett's work of fiction, *The Colour of Magic*:

> Magic had indeed once been wild and lawless, but had been tamed back in the mists of time by the Olden Ones, who had bound it to obey among other things the Law of Conservation of Reality. ... Some of the ancient magic could still be found in its raw state, recognizable – to the initiated – by the eight-fold shape it made in the crystalline structure of space-time. There was the metal octiron, for example, and the gas octogen. Both radiated dangerous amounts of raw enchantment. (1983, p. 60)

Pratchett's literary portrayal of bygone magic, nostalgically recalled from the days of yore, reveals an issue of grappling with an implicit sense of loss in fantasy literature. The "taming" and "binding" of magic by the Olden Ones metaphorically restates the complex relationship between science and magic. While magic was in many ways augmented by its interface with science, which seemed to organize and impart a sense of geometrical efficiency to the raw "wild and lawless" substance of old, this order came at the cost of making it perilous, unstable, and esoterically concealed.

Within the genre of fantasy, arcane, pre-scientific, and superstitious forms of knowledge acquisition are often presented as plausible modes of learning, often functioning even more effectively than the modernized, structured systems. Kroeber sheds light on how fantasy elevates magical sensibilities and sentiments, allowing for inward reflexivity:

> Fantasy emerges out of enlightenment culture, which excluded anything fantastic from civilized life. ... Fantasy celebrates the magical in a society for which magic had become only benighted superstition. The essential mode of Romantic fantastic discourse, therefore, derives from the trope of oxymoron – an impossible possibility. Use of this mode necessarily involves the fantasist in an art of intense self-reflexivity, enchanting himself so that he may enchant others. This inwardness distinguishes fantasy from its nonidentical twin, science fiction. Science fiction appears when the supernatural has been driven out of enlightened society, but instead of seeking to recover otherness and magicality, science fiction extrapolates consequences of the scientific-technological progress that destroyed superstition. (1988, p. 1)

Kroeber discusses the means by which the self, or the idea of the individual, becomes a plane of examination for the magical practitioner. Self-reflexivity and the act of turning inward denies the strict, physical empiricism of scientific study and a rationalist reverence to cause and effect. Kroeber also notes that fantasy seeks to recapture magic and lost aspects of life that were once more aligned with the collective. Quite apart from any specific physical instantiation that magic may or may not have, it is useful in a metaphorical sense as a way to propose a re-engagement with otherness and selfhood. In this way, it becomes a lynchpin for introspection. Kroeber reveals the way that magic reflects a desire that is also present in science fiction, yet which operates quite differently:

> My distinction between science fiction and fantasy exalts neither at the expense of the other. The forms embody two responses to the same historical circumstance, humankind's domination of the natural world so completely that it becomes difficult to conceive of beings other than humans, or of nonhuman modes of existence, or even to imagine what might be termed 'magic,' in the sense of occurrences not answerable to humankind's rational analyses and naturalistic explanations. (1988, p. 24)

Kroeber implies that magic summons a perspective that has become distant to the experience of humankind due to a pervasive domination of the natural world. These visions, of beings other than humans and of nonhuman modes of existence have been eclipsed if not inconceivable. Magic allows for recovery of a lost vision of humankind's relationship with the natural world, cultivating empathy as well. Although this desire is also reflected in science fiction, in its imagination of other futures, the commonality between the two remains only a framework, to imagine new "modes of existence." Kroeber sheds light on how fantasy possesses a unique ability to engender the transformative through language, which becomes an element of enchantment:

> Inwardness, self-reflexivity, and the exploration of self-recursive modes are the characteristics of fantasy. Fantasy responds to the modern conditions of rationalized civilization, culture deprived of enchantment, by seeking to uncover magic possibilities, especially in the processes of linguistic articulation and narratives in themselves. ... To cast a spell, fantasy must be a spell, the texture of its enunciation must be magical, in the sense of bringing forward the amazingly transformative, because self-transformative, powers of language. (1988, pp. 29–30)

Magic is a substance that is highly permeable by language. Spellcasting, as Kroeber notes, requires magical enunciation, and within these processes, the linguistic textures, narratives, and articulations all become generative modes of creation. In this mode, magic closely resembles pedagogy, but allows transformation to occur in a self-reflexive manner. Because it is charged by and with language, magic is powerful in the sense of its ability to interface thought with nature, and this is a recursive process that allows for the self to be transformed.

For Kroeber, the close tie between language and creation found in magic reasserts a lost aspect of humanity and its relationships with environment and will. Kroeber asserts how this recovery is an ongoing process in fantasy:

> Today ... it is fantasy that most rapidly allows us to recover the power of thus using language creatively, to reassert our human power to overcome the strength of human creations which function to dehumanize us by confining us within reified structures of our own making. Fantasy is an enabling mode because it recovers for us a necessary sense that there is something other than ourselves for us to wonder at together. Fantasy opens the marvelous possibility of sharing an expanded sense that there may be more than us and our creations on this earth, that 'more' calling forth the utmost strength of our imagining, such strength being manifested in the necessary complexities of effective human communication. ... It manifests the human power to conceive the inconceivable, the inconceivable being, most simply, whatever is different from the conceiver. And only to the degree that the inconceivable can be communicated, thus becoming common property, can the potency of the truly human be enhanced. (1988, p. 139)

Fantasy's use of magic, consistent within its own structure, becomes a way to open up the possible. Magic becomes a pursuit of fantasy, and in its flowering becomes not only a reminder of the potential to grasp the inconceivable, but even more functions as a road-map for how one can arrive at enchantment.

4   Acquisitions and Transmissions of Magic and Magical Knowledge in Fantasy Literature

Briefly turning an eye to pedagogical representations in fantasy literature, the theme of learning magic is salient, where archetypal characters regularly pose questions and probe into the acquisition and transmission of magic. Witches, wizards, hobgoblins, and fairies frequently size each other up, prying into the source(s) of magical knowledge, investigating this invisible wellspring for friends, foes, or wanderers who unassumingly cross their paths. For example, in C.S. Lewis' *The Chronicles of Narnia, The Lion, the Witch and the Wardrobe*, the White Witch attempts to identify hidden threads of enchantment, asking a magician, "How do you come to know Magic?" (1950, p. 84). More than half a century later, a similar question was posed in Deborah Harkness' *Shadow of Night*: "Who taught you these things. ... From whom did you learn your witchcraft?" (2012, p. 71). In Emily Croy Barker's *The Thinking Woman's Guide to Real Magic*, a similar pedagogical inquiry emerges: "How did you become a magician? ... How hard is it to learn magic? How long before you get to be really good?" (2013, p. 207).

Fantasy literature is rich with pedagogical questions and ruminations on education, and depictions of characters utilizing rituals, spells and other magical devices allowing for encounters with enchanted models of teaching and learning. In Harkness' work, a witch asserts that "Some spells begin with an idea, others with a question. ... Let the power move through you" (2012, p. 331). Teaching is continually emphasized in Harkness' trilogy, and learning outcomes are laid out with necessity in order to overcome malevolence and adversity, although often with vague and uncertain timelines: "We'll teach her what she needs to know. ... It will take her whole life. ... Magic isn't macramé. It takes time" (2011, p. 424). In Lev Grossman's *The Magicians*, a professor stresses the craft and agency of magic:

> The study of magic is not a science, it is not an art, and it is not a religion. Magic is a craft. When we do magic, we do not wish and we do not pray. We rely upon our will and our knowledge and our skill to make a specific change to the world. (2009, p. 48)

In fantasy literature, we are presented with aspects of education that are hyperreal and heightened yet surreal, strange, impossible, and mysterious. The pedagogies of magic establish broad and vexing challenges to the realities that we are familiar with or conscious of in the everyday and in the field of education. If we shall call this realm a field, let us establish a labyrinth with omnidirectional longings, riddled turns, circles, and half circles: a field of education where we may find reflections in the aesthetics of the natural world, a sentiment mirrored often in the realm of the fantastic. At times, let us survey that which is anchored or rootless, nourished by substrate or the atmosphere. Steadying ourselves along hinterland borders, let us glean what we may in search of that nameless enchantment which lurks in the shadows of moss and stone.

While pedagogies in fantasy literature often reflect modes of teaching and learning that at times seem familiar and even mimetic of everyday realities, these are no ordinary lessons or garden labyrinths; they are fantastical and metaphorical spaces that engender enhanced notions of creativity, growth, and embodiment. Generative themes can be seen in statements about the discourse of magical learning in works of fiction, for example, in *Magicians*, by Grossman:

> You need to do more than memorize. … You must learn the principles of magic with more than your head. You must learn them with your bones, with your blood, your liver, your heart. (2009, p. 144)

Magic stretches the possibilities of learning in terms of both techniques and outcomes, and the learning experience entails embodied and metaphysical notions:

> Can you imagine how boring it would be if casting a spell were like turning on an electric drill? But it's not. It's irregular and beautiful. It's not an artifact, it's something else, something organic. It feels like a grown thing, not a made thing. (Grossman, 2009, p. 234)

As opposed to an artificial construction, spellcasting and spell-crafting resemble something mysteriously animated and alive. Open-ended credos hold court, as seen in Patrick Rothfuss' *The Wise Man's Fear*: "It's the questions we can't answer that teach us the most. They teach us how to think" (2011, p. 620). This sentiment of embracing inquiry and complexity is also seen in Harkness' *Shadow of Night*: "And so I discovered that the practice of magic wasn't finding the correct answers but formulating better questions" (2012, p. 340).

5 Archetypes, Transformations, and Transfigurations

The quality of transfiguration relevant in magical knowledge transmission writ large is significant, and openness is a general wind that blows strongly through its vast materials and pedagogies. Yet, there are ways to tame the blowing gales and moor experiences to smaller scales. Archetypes become indispensable here, and the essays in this collection use them as framing mechanisms, allowing for reflections on personal experiences and beyond. These engagements with archetypes both establish and widen the lens of magical pedagogies, as aligned with one's personal interpretations or modes of investigation. It is possible that interfacing with archetypes may alter them to various degrees, as archetypes have established meaning to draw from, but are also conduits to channel new meaning.

According to Jung, archetypes are anchored by ancient elements of mythological lore, yet continuously shape-shift in the current times, as provoked or conjured into existence by the collective unconscious. Jung reflects, "The 'witch' is a collective image" (1971, p. 130). For Jung, archetypal images are variable, manifesting not as fixed elements, but as rhizomes and forms of becoming, capable of shaking off the dust of the past and arising anew. Jung considered archetypes as core elements or seeds, yet with an ability to grow into highly differentiated forms. A metaphor of a crystal's axial system is reflected on by Jung to allow for an apprehension of a system in which archetypes operate:

> It is necessary to point out once more that archetypes are not determined as regards their content, but only as regards their form. ... Its form, however ... might be compared to the axial system of a crystal. ... The archetype in itself is empty and purely formal ... a possibility of representation. ... Our comparison with the crystal is illuminating inasmuch as the axial system determines only the stereometric structure but not the concrete form of the individual crystal. ... The only thing that remains constant is the axial system, or rather, the invariable geometric proportions underlying it. The same is true of the archetype. In principle, it can be named and has an invariable nucleus of meaning – but always only in principle, never in regards it concrete manifestation. (1970, pp. 13–14)

Jung underscores the underlying "axial systems" of archetypes: form may be determined by an implicit pattern of influence, but manifestations and outward representations are variable. For Jung, archetypal images are not tied to resolute states, and the unknown and speculations emerge – overall, an appreciation of the yet-to-be-perceived (or invisible) operates on equal footing with the familiar.

These essays traverse an ultimately ephemeral discourse of mutable archetypal forms, and Jung notes that "an archetypal content expresses itself, first and foremost, in metaphors" (1968, p. 156). They manifest and take on importance in the past and present day: "Archetypes were, and still are, living psychic forces that demand to be taken seriously, and they have a strange way of making sure of their effect" (1968, pp. 156–157). The Jungian process involves entering into and interpreting an open terrain of dream, myth, personal, and collective imagery:

> Clear-cut distinctions and strict formulations are quite impossible in this field, seeing that a kind of fluid interpenetration belongs to the very nature of all archetypes. They can only be roughly circumscribed at best. Their living meaning comes out more from their presentation as a whole than from a single formulation. Every attempt to focus them more sharply is immediately punished by the intangible core of meaning

> losing its luminosity. No archetype can be reduced to a simple formula. It is a vessel which we can never empty, and never fill. It has a potential existence only, and when it takes shape in matter it is no longer what it was. It persists throughout the ages and requires interpreting ever anew. (Jung, 1968, p. 179)

The investigative and experimental approaches of these essays necessitate and reinforce openness in exploring whether archetypes each present their own models and limits as to the manner in which magic and pedagogies form or define them. Perhaps the spirit of this collective investigation, to borrow a phrase from Jung, is aligned with the quest of "ferreting out possibilities" of each archetype and the potential connection to magic and pedagogies (1971, p. 224).

Jung's life-long inspection of archetypes includes what he calls a "primordial image," or "archetypal image," noting that these images may be both variable and "ever-enduring" (1971, p. 321). The generative and imaginative impulse of "activating them," in the light of the present day offers a wellspring of meaning, and their existence perhaps serves a purpose in counteracting that which may be lacking:

> The impact of an archetype, whether it takes the form of immediate experience or is expressed through the spoken word, stirs us because it summons up a voice that is stronger than our own. Whoever speaks in primordial images speaks with a thousand voices; he enthrals and overpowers, while at the same time he lifts the idea he is seeking to express out of the occasional and the transitory into the realm of the ever-enduring. ... The creative process, so far as we are able to follow it at all, consists in the unconscious activation of an archetypal image, and in elaborating and shaping the image into the finished work. By giving it shape, the artist translates it into the language of the present, and so makes it possible for us to find our way back to the deepest springs of life. Therein lies the social significance of art: it is constantly at work educating the spirit of the age, conjuring up the forms in which the age is most lacking. (Jung, 1971, p. 321)

For Jung, this chorus of "a thousand voices" is a lasting and sensible aspect of the collective mythic past and is essential to art making. It involves selfhood and personal agency, allowing one to channel or transform the transitory into the ever enduring. Using Jungian modes, we may be selective in the infinite and changeable field of archetypal images, actively observing what is useful,

INTRODUCTION   19

gleaning what is tangible, and understanding that there is more than meets the eye to be reckoned with and possibly discovered.

Through the study of folklore, myth, dreams, and art, Jung's lifelong studies often interface with fantasy. Like archetypes, the trope of fantasy is in itself as liminal and nimble, for the most part situated neither here nor there, requiring interpretation and oftentimes a heavy dose of poetic speculation. This hinterland of the in-between provokes reflection. If meaning and concrete objectives are to be found and reckoned with, it is alongside ambiguity and prismatic hesitation.

Northrop Frye's investigation of images and archetypes illustrate the poetic nuances of metaphor, language, and tropes, paving the way for pluralistic insights. Frye also unveils the way that literature interfaces with magic:

> The long-standing connection between the written book and the arts of magic, and the way that the poetic impulse seems to begin in the renunciation of magic, or at least, of its practical aims. ... The written word is far more powerful than simply a reminder: it re-creates the past in the present, and gives us, not the familiar remembered thing, but the glittering intensity of the summoned-up hallucination. (1982, p. 227)

Frye's practice of examining literature through its embedded imagery becomes poetically expanded in his claims about magic. By indicating that magic conjures a mirage, recreates, and reimagines, the mythopoeic is elevated as a determinant of intensity and creative agency.

Frye suggests that the recurring images in literature are archetypes with familiar associative properties capable of being both recognized and communicated:

> Archetypes are associative clusters, and differ from signs in being complex variables. Within the complex is often a large number of specific learned associations which are communicable because a large number of people in a given culture happen to be familiar with them. (1957, p. 102)

Frye perceives mythic structures as markers for the limits of possible imaginings, illustrating desire:

> We begin our study of archetypes, then, with a world of myth, an abstract or purely literary world of fictional and thematic design, unaffected by canons of plausible adaptation to familiar experience. In terms of narrative, myth is the imitation of actions near or at the conceivable limits of desire. (1957, p. 136)

Through an archetypal lens, we may investigate the manner in which pedagogical motifs interplay with myth and desire. Because they operate near the "limits of conceivable desire," archetypes allow for radical departures from normative models, leaving behind the shackles of the merely convenient, routine, or realistic.

In *Fantasy: The Literature of Subversion*, Rosemary Jackson theorizes how modes of fantasy interface with ideas of desire and absence. She reflects on the complex scope and allure of fantasy:

> Fantasy, both in literature and out of it, is an enormous and seductive subject. Its association with imagination and with desire has made it an area difficult to articulate or to define, and indeed the 'value' of fantasy has seemed to reside in precisely this resistance to definition, in its 'free-floating' and escapist qualities. (1981, p. 1)

Although fantasy is elusive and escapes crystallization, it is not fruitless to inspect certain aspects of how the fantastic may manifest, fade, and reappear again, like fungi after a rain. Both fantasy and archetypes deal with desire as the quest of searching, detecting, interpreting, and noticing come into play.

6   Archetypes, Magic, and Knowledge

Archetypes and models of magical knowledge are myriad in this collection of essays, with no shortage of metaphors within their folds. The potency of the field of fantasy is that it allows for models of magical inquiry and learning to be present in vast varieties, where boundaries and borders are neither fixed nor beholden to consistencies, and the archetypes in residence among these pages inhabit this vastness. However, archetypes grant a significant vessel of storytelling about educational models that can illuminate real-world potential for enhanced reflections. Not only can archetypes reveal patterns, but ideally convey resonant personal meaning that paves the way for humanistic reflections, beckoning us to view education under an overall idiosyncratic and widened lens. Magic is perhaps not harder won than other forms of knowledge, but it does enable a mythopoeic imagination to be applied to education, enhancing ideas of transformation, empathy, selfhood, wonder, and creativity.

Upon turning attention to our own paths, perhaps we may determine which archetypal models resonate and hold meaning for us, including past educational trajectories and desired roads ahead. Or, perhaps it is valuable to perceive these archetypes operating in equilibrium with one another within any educational trajectory, each surfacing and existing on their own terms, with their own quirky tenets to reckon with. Or, our own archetypal icons, inspirations, or identities may be a chimera of self-chosen qualities. Ideally, artful and fantastical portals may open and close at our own choosing as we identify possibilities in the face of persistent strangeness, cope with untold challenges, see beyond permeable distortions, and forge ahead in this present day labyrinth with omnidirectional longings. Within this collection, there is no culmination of answers about magic and no single weathervane surrounding its discourse. Yet, a weird spigot of humanization flows from enchantment, wielding artistic influences and inviting newness to confront the unknown.

Acknowledgement

This chapter contains parts of Razdow, K. A. (2004). *Enchanted pedagogy: Archetypal forms, magic, and the transmission of knowledge in fantasy literature* [Unpublished Ed.D. dissertation]. Teachers College, Columbia University.

References

Barker, E. C. (2013). *The thinking woman's guide to real magic*. Viking.
Briggs, K. (1962). *Pale Hecate's team*. Routledge & Kegan Paul Limited.
Dewey, J. (1916). *Democracy and education*. The Free Press.
Freire, P. (1970). *Pedagogy of the oppressed*. Continuum International Publishing Group.
Frye, N. (1957). *Anatomy of criticism*. Princeton University Press.
Frye, N. (1982). *The great code: The Bible and literature*. Houghton Mifflin Harcourt Publishing Group.
Greene, M. (2001). *Variations on a blue guitar*. Teachers College Press.
Grossman, L. (2009). *The magicians*. Penguin Group.
Harkness, D. (2011). *A discovery of witches*. Penguin Books.
Harkness, D. (2012). *Shadow of night*. Penguin Books.
Jackson, R. (1981). *Fantasy: The literature of subversion*. Routledge.
Jung, C. G. (1968). *The archetypes and the collective unconscious*. Princeton University Press.
Jung, C. G. (1970). *Four archetypes*. Princeton University Press.
Jung, C. G. (1971). *The portable Jung* (J. Campbell, Ed.). Viking Press.
Kroeber, K. (1988). *Romantic fantasy and science fiction*. Yale University Press.
Le Guin, U. K. (2004). From Elfland to Poughkeepsie. In D. Sandner (Ed.), *Fantastic literature: A critical reader* (pp. 144–155). Praeger Publishers.

Lewis, C. S. (1950). *The chronicles of Narnia, the lion, the witch, and the wardrobe*. HarperCollins.

Mauss, M. (1972). *A general theory of magic*. Routledge.

Pratchett, T. (1983). *The colour of magic*. St. Martin's Press.

Rothfuss, P. (2011). *The wise man's fear*. Daw Books, Inc.

CHAPTER 2

Huldufólk

Jesse Bransford

If you have ever been to Iceland, chances are you have been told about the huldufólk. The so-called 'hidden people' of Icelandic folklore have roots in the larger northern European tales of the fairy and elven realms. What many visitors are surprised by when confronted with the huldufólk is the matter-of-factness with which they are discussed. Credulous or no, the subject almost always arises when talking about the character of the land, of Iceland the place. A simplification to explain the persistence of this folkloric attitude would be one of personification: Iceland the place has a personality, and the huldufólk lend themselves quite easily to this persona.

The huldufólk are specific to Iceland and the Faroe Islands, but they clearly sit within a larger cultural history and mythology that describe a race of beings like humans, but occupying a separate realm, a magical space charmed, without the fears and concerns of the normal world. Their origin stories are varied, but these beings are seen as close to us as a people but closer still to the natural order and the unseen forces of magic and the land.

The hidden people exist in a realm that overlaps with our own, a sci-fi space akin to 'here,' only out of phase and invisible to our limited perception. What we do has direct implications in the lands of the huldufólk: our space is their space, despite the differences. Children are warned not to throw rocks wantonly: one might strike a hidden person. Many stone outcroppings are described as 'elf homes' and are considered with reverence and respect. The joining of terrain visible to land invisible here is a powerful device. These tales, among other things, are an allegory of the unseen, a reminder that our eyes only tell a partial story of what is actually in front of us, and furthermore that much of what we 'see' is 'made.' It also reminds us that we share our confines with myriad entities, many of which exist outside the range of our normal senses. These are a timeless set of concerns, and are vital to survival, now more than ever.

In a contemporary Icelandic setting, travelers are jokingly told to beware of the huldufólk and trolls when out in the wilds. They are the tales of warning for children (and tourists), but with a less-than-joking edge, mostly, I'd imagine, to underline the real dangers of exposure in the Icelandic countryside.

This warning at the edge of civilization is one I've received in several parts of the world, and I think of the 'little people' (as they are also known) in a wider pan-cultural context. Seeing the folkloric persistence of elven folk in our views of nature is telling; there is a kernel of wisdom at the boundary between the world and what we make of it. The folkloric here is a perpetual reminder that mastery is only ever partial and that for every act, every action, there are consequences that come into focus, often long after the fact. Control and understanding are fixed in time, and time moves.

On the Icelandic coast of Strandir, certainly one of the most remote places remaining on the planet Earth, I have been told many stories about the 'little people.' They are everywhere in Strandir, I was told, and even considering the stories from the most metaphorical standpoint, I would hesitate to disagree: as empty and elemental as the land is, it is unquestionably alive. But, because so little of the life is near us in morphology, the way life moves is almost always just out of our field of normal vision: too small to focus on, too slow to track. Everything seems to do its work just outside our frame of reference. And yet this chthonic energy is everywhere felt, a sense of immensity, profundity: from the clouds, the wind, the rocks that vent steam. 'How does one see the invisible?' I was asked rhetorically one early but dark October evening outside the hamlet of Drangsnes. You must sit and stare, I was told, certainly for no less than a full day. Stare in silent stillness, for if you move the vision will falter. If you are successful, so the story unfolded, the hidden realm will emerge, and the beings will communicate secrets. Akvavit helps, I was told with a wink and a nod.

Sitting writing in the Village of Catskill, I think of the tale of Rip Van Winkle, who wandering into a chance encounter with some of the little people, lent a helping hand with a barrel of savory liquor. A glass for his trouble before returning home enables the story of a comedic and portentous loss of time. Washington Irving of course knew the traditional fairy literature he was referring to, and while from a literary standpoint the tale is clearly of an Irish or Scottish cast, the setting is specific and purposeful; the landscape of the Catskills lends easily to the cast of such tales. The glacial mountains have a majesty and mystery that suggest the sense of chthonic wonder and respect these tales emerge from. They *speak* to us.

Classical anthropology has generally turned these stories into reflexive gestures, casting the tales as stories of one culture's push to the social boundary by another, remembered as folk tales that subsume the vanquished clan into the wilderness and the anxieties of the 'outside' from the 'inside.' The value for us here is the idea of 'outside' as it pertains to the 'inside' as a site of understanding: if anthropology has a place of continued relevance it will acknowledge that the boundary of interior and exterior is a place of eternal speculation and controversy. The terms by which we define interior and exterior can easily be moved to create a more novel set of considerations and speculations.

The fairy folk we know through Disney tales and anthropological rationalizations are a much altered genus of creature from almost all of the folkloric records. Tolkien's contemporary mythology is a rare example that preserves somewhat the essence of the elven tales of folklore. Aloof, retiring, and sovereign in their own terms, the huldufólk of myth have only strained relations with our lumbering and myopic ways. In political terms, it is a fragile peace, more of a treaty of non-belligerence, and one that if transgressed carries sore consequences for the transgressor. In many tales, strong penalties are levied for crossing into the fairy realm, and those who return are permanently changed, for better or worse, touched by the power of the Tuatha Dé Danann...

I'm mixing terms purposefully in an attempt to show just how endemic the idea of huldufólk are to our thoughts about story and nature. Scientist and mythologist Jacques Vallée has contributed a body of work that suggests the pan-cultural context I bring to bear on the huldufólk: his contention, still quite novel in the world of UFO speculation, is that our modern perception of the extraterrestrial alien is the most recent envisioning of an uninterrupted history of shared existence with non-human consciousness, consciousness that presents often in terms that strongly resemble the huldufólk mythology. Loss of time, strange, often humorous and dreamlike narratives, an interest in our reproductive energies and our offspring, and finally, among a paraphrased list of characteristics, the often diminutive, lithe, and luminous quality these beings have to our senses. The common stories, across place and time, beg questions of a larger context, a moved edge of the boundary between inside and out.

The huldufólk here are the voice of the natural order. In the simplest formulation, they are the communicators of the language of nature. Their ambivalence towards us is matched only by the wrath with which they course-correct our stumblings through the evolutionary boundaries of time. This is not to separate us from nature, it gives voice to the relationship. Are they 'real'? This is the wrong question. They are inescapable, and this is independent of their scientific reality. Inescapable in that we will always formulate relations of consciousness and agency to what is not us. We should. To give them voice, or rather to listen is a choice we make or do not at our own peril.

References

Bates, B. (1983). *Tales of an Anglo-Saxon sorcerer: The way of the wyrd*. Book Club Associates.

Hallmundsson, M., & Hallmundsson, H. (2014). *Icelandic folk and fairy tales*. Forlagið.

Larrington, C. (2017). *The Norse myths: A guide to the gods and heroes*. Thames & Hudson.

Larrington, C. (Trans.) (2019). *The Poetic Edda*. Oxford University Press.

McKenna, T. (1993). *True hallucinations: Being an account of the author's extraordinary adventures in the devil's paradise*. Harper.

Rolleston, T. W. (1986). *Myths and legends of the Celtic race*. Shocken Books.

Sigmundsdóttir, A. (2015). *The little book of the hidden people*. Enska textasmidjan.

Simpson, J. (2009). *Icelandic folktales & legends*. History Press.

Smith, C. A. (2015). *Icelandic magic: Aims, tools and techniques of the Icelandic sorcerers*. Avalonia.

Tolkien, J. R. R. (2014). *The Silmarillion*. Mariner Books.

Vallée, J. (1988). *Dimensions: A casebook of alien contact*. Contemporary Books.

CHAPTER 3

Shedding Skins

Vanessa Chakour

> *Stories of the Selkies, the seal people from rural coastal communities of Scotland, Ireland, and Iceland, are often told as stories of longing. They are stories of separation from home, from nature, from community. Some are tales of domestication, losing oneself in love, and longing for the freedom of the wild. They speak to a gnawing ache for home, for our animal nature, for who we really are.*
>
> *In order for a selkie to come ashore, they must shed their seal skin and transform for a time, into humans. And if one managed to find a selkie's skin and hide it away, the seal person could not return to sea. Many of the tales about selkie folk have been collected from the Northern Isles of Scotland where many of my ancestors are from. Some of those people, legends say, have seal blood running through their veins.*

It was autumn in New England. As days grew darker earlier and earlier, light barely glimmered into the bedroom. It was just three weeks after we met but time was irrelevant. You felt familiar, like I'd always known you, or maybe, had been waiting for you. Whatever it was, I found the courage to get lost.

In those dreamy days, we came up for air to hike among fiery colors of dying leaves. We hunted for mushrooms – maitake, chicken of the woods, turkey tail – sea creatures of the forest floor. You, determined, scanned the edges of trails and found them. I infused our morning coffees, soups and stews with our bounty and as we sipped and ate, we searched for the right words to share our deepest thoughts, ideas, dreams and desires. We wanted to expose ourselves, to be seen, to offer each other a nakedness beyond our skin.

Selkies are shapeshifters who, like us, live in worlds beneath the waves. They swim above and below water, giving them the ability to experience both the inner and outer worlds. In folklore, shape-shifting speaks to worlds where boundaries between humans and nature do not exist. These stories are less about affirming our separation from the other animals than remembering that we are part of them. And we are, in fact, related to the creatures of forests, meadows and oceans and even to the maple trees and wildflowers outside our doors. But when we forget that we are related, that we crawled from the same ocean, there is an ache, a longing for 'home' that is just beyond our reach.

Nine months later, it is summer. Bright rays of sun pierce our sleep and pour into our bed through the skylight. We wake in this new space, squinting, and smile at each other. You caress me gently and kiss me wherever you find my star-kissed skin – my back, my forehead, my shoulder. You remind me that these photons, these beams of light that touch me, are incredibly precious, *they may have been waiting, bouncing around for 100,000 years inside the core of the sun, waiting to reach you.* I know that all life on Earth is nourished by this committed star. I also know that suns and stars engulf their planets, eventually. Sometimes I think I will burn up, be consumed by you too.

That day, I was preparing to guide, 'Animism and Ecology in Gaelic Lore,' an online class with friend Àdhamh Ó Broin, when I told you the story of the Selkie Wife.

> Some tales say that on an autumn night, under a full moon, a lonely fisherman wandered along the edge of the ocean and came upon beautiful women dancing in the moonlight. Stunned by their beauty, he hid behind a large rock to watch them and as he did, his lonely heart awakened and he fell in love. While one of the selkie women was lost in ecstasy, he stole her skin knowing that without it, she could not return home.
>
> Soon, the moonlight faded, the sun rose and her sisters dove back into the sea. The lone selkie was frantic, searching everywhere for her skin. She was desperate, naked, and in tears when the fisherman finally revealed himself. With no one else to turn to, she begged him for help. But instead of giving her the seal skin, and a choice, he hid it, professed his love and promised to take care of her if she married him. Tragically, she had no other choice.
>
> The seal woman began a domesticated life and in time, accepted her circumstances, learned to be somewhat happy, and even enjoyed a loving relationship with her captor, the fisherman, with whom she bears children. Some stories say she had a close relationship with her daughter and others, her son. But despite any joy, there was always part of her that was longing, gazing out at sea, while the fisherman, preoccupied with hiding her skin, checked and double-checked his locks, to be sure his selkie wife would not flee.

We spoke about the restlessness that comes with being in a space too small, a relationship too confining and the ache that comes with knowing we have to leave. In New York City, in 2019, I was in the wrong environment, in a relationship with a sweet man for too long. I found this excerpt in my journal:

I'm making money to spend money to go nuts in a tiny little box and to go home and stare into a tiny little box when there is a massively magical and expansive world out there. I'm ripe, bearing fruit but all the juices just spill on the floor here, and I have to clean them up. They should be soaked up by the soil, food for the flora, food for the chaos of life.

Not long afterward, I found my seal skin and left.

After a while, as her children grow, she grows listless. Her skin becomes dry and flaky, and her loving child is concerned. The selkie mother cannot bear it anymore and tells her daughter the story. Wanting to heal her beloved mom, she searches for the skin. After many years, her daughter goes fishing with her father and finds the skin hidden away in a chest. There are variations on this tale – sometimes the fisherman doesn't even know about the skin – but in all stories, when the selkie wife discovers her seal skin, her freedom, she is faced with a gut-wrenching decision. She loves her child, even came to love the husband who captured her, but she cannot resist the call of the wild. She throws on the skin, says goodbye, and returns to the sea.

Some say that the selkie wife swam with her children by the shore, or that they were seen playing with a large seal. Others say although she loved her family, she was never seen again.

Eleven months later, you make me a breakfast of miso soup filled with all of our leftovers – kale stalks, shiitake mushrooms, carrots, onion, foraged greens; the entire vegetable drawer. You brush my hair as I write and insist on buying detangler for my knotted mane so we shop at the Coop and you roam the aisles with such earnest patience, reading labels, clipping coupons. At night you ask probing questions, turning things over and over and over in your mind. You say you are proud of me, excited about my writing and work when I doubt myself.

But still, I get lost in you. We are melding into each other, trying to find our way.

We both have our fears that we will leave each other, in different ways: I am hyper-aware of impermanence, of the fragility of life, and am afraid that something unexpected might happen to you. You are afraid that I will wake up one day out of the trance of love and leave you. That I will find my 'seal skin' and just ... go.

Now, it is almost a year and we are apart for some weeks so I can focus and write. The act of creativity, like falling in love, is another kind of freedom, and another kind of endless abyss. It is healing work that loosens something inside me, allows me to dive deep and hear parts of the self that have not been available to my conscious mind. And in order to get there, I need time and space to swim alone. But without you, this big bed feels like an ocean.

I sleep, and as I dream, I search for my skin, trying to find the part of me that you have claimed. Like the selkie, I looked everywhere, panicked. But when I look in the mirror, my skin is still there, intact. It was always there. You didn't steal it, you never would. And really, you never could. I got lost of my own volition and I am different now. My life has shapeshifted, I have shapeshifted. I have different expectations, different needs, different desires. I used to believe I couldn't have both love and freedom, yet your love freed me.

In order to fall, we must surrender. Love strips away at any and all false veneers toward our core; the essence of who we are. We lose ourselves, forget ourselves and eventually land on solid ground – with our beloved or without – and the 'us' we remember is not quite the same.

Within each of us, I believe there is an 'inner wild', an inner knowing about who we are, an ocean of memory where we remember that we are related to all that is wild. Our seal skin is always there, ready to be found, waiting to be reclaimed.

Yet sometimes, we need to come ashore and take the risk, and shed our skins.

CHAPTER 4

The Gnome Report from Mother Lode Country

Trinie Dalton

Cats and rabbits
Would reside in fancy little houses
And be dressed in shoes and hats and trousers
In a world of my own

All the flowers
Would have very extra-special powers
They would sit and talk to me for hours
When I'm lonely in a world of my own

There'd be new birds
Lots of nice and friendly how-de-do birds
Everyone would have a dozen blue birds

Within that world of my own
I could listen to a babbling brook
And hear a song that I could understand

I keep wishing it could be that way
Because my world would be a wonderland

(*In a World of My Own* lyrics from Alice in Wonderland)

Tiny *but* mighty, why *but*? Isn't but an insult? Invisibility is something a lot of folx I know generally rail against. In social justice movements, or anything interested in equity really, raising awareness is fundamentally dependent on increasing visibility. The causes and conditions surrounding underrepresentation are widely researched and discussed, but rarely is the end-goal in itself: to be seen. *Of course* it's best to be seen. Isn't it? That's survival of the fittest. David Attenborough's copious lifetime coverage of birds of paradise proves that there's no evolution – no survival – without visibility. Attraction, and the competitions it spawns, is reproduction's keystone. Bling is a good thing.
    Unless you're a gnome.

Secret Joy is one of the Gnome's lessons. Gnomes are ascetics, witches, medicine makers, generating everything from regular chores to surprise treats, behind the scenes. Monks, nuns, and yogis. A gnome creates auxiliary spaces – opportunities – that we don't initially see, didn't previously know, maybe didn't exist. Gnome is epiphany. Gnome is psychotropic. Gnome's requests for support, often resembling demands and threats, activate mutual aid and reciprocity: put out the leather for your shoes OR ELSE. Feed that statue some shou-tao (longevity peach) OR ELSE. If your farm's tomten wants to give their milk allotment to the fox that just tried to steal your chickens (as in Astrid Lundgren's *The Tomten and the Fox*) you best be letting them give your hard-earned gifts away freely. If Heinzelmännchen bake your bread and spice your meat because they are masochistic German Protestant work-ethics incarnate, then by all means let them flavor that savory pie. Don't work any little helpers to the bone: if they're out toiling too often, like Snow White's dwarves, their protective charms may weaken and predators will take advantage of this. I wonder if Disney's *Snow White* for all of its Capitalist mining overtones and troublesome gender cliches, is actually an anti-chore tale about how too much labor damages family intimacy. Disrupting new formations of love not only wrecks humans, but entire ecosystems. Where love grows, stay put. If anyone tries to tell you that garden gnomes are there to police productivity, remind them that productivity's Janus head to charisma + sustenance is relaxation + romance. In this, garden gnomes are akin to scarecrows who shoo off busy bodies. Kitsch and folk art usually have lucky charms built right into them, isn't this John Berger idea, maybe from his essay "The White Bird." Here's a beginner's list of chore-oriented, humanoid Gnomes, not including malevolent goblin-types and larger non-humanoid cryptids:

Hob (England), Lutin (French), Otek (Germanic), Domovoi (Russian), Far Darrig (Irish), Klaubautermann & Erdmanleins (German), Nisse (Norway), Tontti (Finnish), Foddenskkmaend (Icelandic), Dudje (Bulgaria), Skritek (Belgian), Mano (Hungary), Kleinmanneken (Swiss), Di sma (Swedish), Dokkaebi (Korea), Duende (Iberian, Philipino), Ebu gogo (Indonesia), Egbere (Yoruba), Iratxo (Basque), Twlwyth teg (Wales), Alux / Chanekeh, Chaneque (Mayan/Aztec).

Gnome, as talisman, sorts it out, doesn't like oversimplification; like a hormonal teenager, Gnome doesn't like to explain. Gnome, like most Cryptids, Monsters, and Demigods, embodies uncertainty and change.

In exchange for my acceptance of uncertainty, Gnome nurtures me by reminding me that invisible help "from the universe" exists, and where it doesn't, it can be sculpted. Gnomes carry the water, as my Poetry colleague Sara Borjas says. Gnome is Gaia energy, lava flow. In the 16th century, Paracelsus assigned Earth elements to Gnomes:

THE GNOME REPORT FROM MOTHER LODE COUNTRY

> In folklore, gnomes are subterranean spirits who guard the earth's treasures. In psychological terms they symbolize whatever is keeping you from your task of entering and getting to know your unconscious (= earth) so as to discover your inner, true self (= treasure). According to the Kabbalah gnomes were genii, short in stature, who lived underground and possessed treasures of precious metals and jewels.
>
> Their legend travelled from the Near East to Scandinavia and to Central America. They came to symbolize the invisible being who by inspiration, intuition, imagination or in dream makes visible things which are invisible. They exist within the human soul as flashes of knowledge, enlightenment or revelation. They are, as it were, the hidden soul of things, whether organic or not, and when they leave them those things die, become lifeless and shadowy. Gnomes are fickle and can swiftly change from loving to hating a person. Slowly gnomes grew in the imagination into ugly, misshapen, malign and evil dwarfs. On the other hand their womenfolk, although even smaller, were dazzlingly beautiful and wore long pointed slippers, one ruby, the other emerald. The pair, or the gnome duplicated as a male and female complex, symbolizes the conjunction in all beings of the beautiful and the ugly, good and evil, dark and light. Undoubtedly they are images of complex and fleeting states of consciousness in which knowledge co-exists with ignorance, moral wealth with moral poverty. They are examples of the conjunction of opposites and of knowledge held in secret or hidden.
>
> The symbol has no connection with gnomic poetry except a common derivation from the Greek gignoskein, 'to perceive.' (dreamicus, 2023)

Gnome has always been fundamental to my artist goals, teacher goals, personhood. Facilitator, instigator, host. Actively engaged fly on the wall. Rockhound, collector of shiny things. Storytelling trader, conversation merchant. Help humans who want help, otherwise help others in need, like pollinators. Tentacular thinking, per Donna Haraway's (2016) definition. This is an incredibly difficult, unstable, and weirdly expensive path to walk. I just have no idea how to do it. In continually uncovering stories of my relatives who were addicts, rapists, robbers, prostitutes, and abusers, I focus on the survivor tales that my parents rescued from that corrosion. I aspire to so much more. Working hard on dissipating shame. Trading tips with classroom discourse communities about how to write it into stories, and out of our bodies, has always been the primary goal. Storytellers, as we all know, too often bring piles of guilt and shame to the table and work it out through revising and inventing characters, plots, settings. Shine the light on shame, share it, and suddenly we see we aren't alone. Guilt vanishes when visibility is encouraged, particularly in learning spaces.

The gnome's paradox, for me, is that visibility demands hierarchy. Doesn't it, inevitably, whether it wants to or not? I mean, it's one thing for advertising to exploit that notion, but I'm talking more about biology and phenomenology. Occupation of space – materialization – precludes natural order. Humans transform that assembly line into laws codified through hieratic script, taxonomy, and religion. But before humans muck it up, everyone and everything is born. Conception, the moment it happens, implies certain classifications, doesn't it? Conception, for a surviving fetus, is followed by a stamp of health. Nature and Chaos are both brilliant detectives. Wanna be a buddha but can never be a buddha. Why is life on earth set up that way? Why is equality impossible? Why do the laws of nature champion presence? Mythologies tell us that cruel gods punish because a few peeps broke taboos. Forgiveness, salvation, and redemption are frequently merit badges in cosmogony tales. Why do we eternally have to pay the price for old mistakes? Well for starters, burial's chemistry is based on decomposition, resuscitation, and rearrangement. Hydrogen, oxygen, nitrogen, carbon don't just vanish. H_2O doesn't just evaporate. When you're a Gnome, you're constantly exposing intergenerational trauma to inform new material. Storytelling begets storytelling; it's Gnome's materia medica. Visibility that heals is essential. But beware Capitalism's commodification of pride, which breeds ego.

If visibility is Capitalism's number one requirement, what good are metaphysical hangovers like the humanities? Academic Administrations ask me this, directly, with alarming frequency these days. What if I release ego in favor of uplifting my family relations and honoring relatives by ending the crap they endured? When do essential workers get a raise? Repatriation. Remediation. Worms, ants, bacteria, maggots: aerators and decomposers surely deserve better. Larger paychecks, larger composts. #LandBack. *You need more gnomes in your life*, I think, during school meetings when critical thinking skills are on the educational chopping block.

Gnomes, as apparitions, understand that critical thinking can't happen without circular memory. I think I understand why Paracelsus assigned Gnomes to all things solid and terrestrial (Faena, 2023). Ghosts surround us whether we like it or not. They're built into all the fabrics and mineral structures that we rely upon for shelter. If we honor them, they give us passes. Haunting happens when we try to dismiss, erase, or obscure their efforts to materialize reminders. For this idea filtered through Classicism and Architectural Theory, I recommend Christian Norberg-Schulz's (1979, p. 18) book, *Genius Loci: Towards a Phenomenology of Architecture*:

> Genius loci [spirit of place] is a Roman concept...every 'independent' being has its genius, its guardian spirit. This spirit gives life to people and

places, accompanies them from birth to death, and determines character or essence...The genius thus denotes a thing that is, or what it 'wants to be'.

If genius is our guardian spirit – or spirits, let's pluralize that – then it is imperative to acknowledge, welcome, and listen to ghosts. There's that call for visibility again ....

I had the privilege of working with many ghosts on a former Montpelier, Vermont Civil War Hospital site for a decade. Built in 1864, it accommodated up to 500 patients, staff, and guards. It was designed with the "pavilion principle" in mind, influenced by Florence Nightingale's calls for sunlight, clear circulating air, and calming views. This meant several buildings instead of a single massive structure, and smaller treatment wards with an abundance of windows and ventilators. Her studies on how many "pints of moisture" humans emit, and how unhealthy confined soil smothering beneath floorboards can be, and how earth and light work together – or antagonistically – to heal, are brilliant (Boone & Sherman, 2001). After the war, the site became a Methodist Seminary in 1866, and majestic College Hall (National Park Service, n.d.) – an impeccable example of Second Empire Baroque style architecture (Sidler, 2019) – was built from 1868–1872. It has served education since that date. As a site of healing and learning, it remains full of spirit. Anyway, Vermont College of Fine Arts, whose writing residencies were my second home for many years, housed me in big empty buildings for weeks at a time, which I loved despite the loneliness. I moved between a brick Greek Revival dormitory renovated with midcentury modern cinderblock; a 1929 Dutch Revival gambrel house; and a 1900 American Farmhouse with colonial flair. I could hear every spirit! I wrote a story imagining that one was Eazy E. with long purple E.T. fingers, when he stopped through. Footsteps, doors, cabinets, occupied basements. Some of the campus's spirits have names, like Anna. Consensus is that they're all benevolent. This acceptance of mysterious cohabitation meant that when there were signs that unhoused people were sneaking into unlocked dorm rooms down the halls from me to avoid freezing to death during icy winters, I wasn't too afraid of crime. I was just glad the buildings were still doing their jobs.

During these years, I concurrently studied how rocks and minerals hold energy and how miners who immigrate to excavate get heavy doses of these vibes. Hope Cemetery in Barre, Vermont is packed with granite carved by Italian immigrants who worked the quarry in Graniteville, and don't even get me started on Vermont's Danby marbles. I hand-carried home by airplane a very heavy, thrift-scored, variegated rose and white marble lamp from Vermont Marble Company, which I still read by nightly. Have spent copious amounts of time staring at and rubbing Vermont state building exteriors, even once interviewed another Vermont marble fan about how Vermont's *verde antique* – a deep creamy green "marble" – is really a serpentine quarried an hour north of Danby. Left a few purchased tombstone scraps in Vermont when I got pregnant: husband said to stop carrying rocks on airplanes. Fast forward through four years of Mojave desert basin-and-range geology forays to study flowering plant affinities for soils, rocks, and minerals; two trips into Slovenian (Veness & Veness, 2015) and Croatian (Bousfield, 2022) travertine-rich Karst topography for Slavic mythology research; and now, finally, relocation to Mother Lode Country, where my office now sits on top of an abandoned gold mine called Baby Consolidated. It's part of the Idaho-Maryland quartz-gold complex, once the most lucrative Gold Rush site in California and now threatening to re-open (MineWatch Coalition, 2023). I drive past Centennial Site daily and worry when its windy that old arsenic dust may blow in my car windows (Branson-Potts, 2022). See? Burying waste just doesn't work. Out of sight is not out of mind. But I mostly dream of gorgeous tunnels and caves beneath my feet, sparkling with crystals strewn with metals of every color. I feel super lucky, who wouldn't, and want it all to remain in-ground.

While rock and mineral vibrations are the subject of ten future essays, I mention this to connect Paracelsus's understanding of Gnome's subterranean roles. Gnomes are not simply ghosts. Gnomes are the O.G. mine and cave-dwelling Treasurers. It's their job to monitor Earth's balance and flow. They are stewards. A recent trip to Virginia City, Nevada got me thinking that the Comstock Lode is likely overpopulated not only by miners' ghosts but by all sorts of Gnomes. In other words, in mining regions Gnomes live down there with, or below, the ghosts of men who perished in mining accidents. It's a thing. Slavic myth has Karzelek, guardian of gems, crystals, and precious metals. Nevada County, California has Cornish Tommyknockers, Coblynau occupy Welsh mines, Muki is a duende who guard mines in the Andes.

The point is: Paracelsus, in an era when mysticism and science still overlapped, knew as well as any cosmology tale (one would guess) that earth and air are intrinsically connected by water. Water creates the underground pockets where rare beauty grows, particularly where its surrounding substrates trade minerals with it. If water is the lifeline between air and water, then, doesn't that mean that the Gnome archetype is water itself? The responsibility we have to tend water? Gnome holds memory like water, envelopes subterranean treasures, connects below to above. Gnome maintains, witnesses, preserves. Let's just go all the way here: was Gnome, before he became the symbol of extraction, the original environmental activist? Water protector? If I'm sleuthing back to pre-Christian pagan and indigenous thinking, Gnomes weren't little people. They were places where water spoke to us because water is our ancestor. We are water, and water is us. Here's a beginner's list of tiny but mighty spirits: mercurial wisdom holders, ancestral spirits who connect human to natural elements through guardianship, tricksterism, mischief, etc.:

Ta'ai (Taiwanese), Eloko (Mondo-Nkundo people, Central Africa), Aziza (Dahomey people, Nigeria), Memehune (Hawaiian), Nirumbee or Awwakkulé (Crow) Nimerigar (Shoshone), Jogah (Iriquois), Čanotila (Lakota), Yehasuri (Catawba), Yunwi Tsunsdi (Cherokee), Kowi Anukasha (Choctaw), Pukwudgie (Wampanoag), Memegwesi (Anishinaabe, Ojibwe), Kiwolatomuhsisok (Maliseet), Makiawisug (Mohegan).

Decolonization is (freakin' finally) a buzzword amongst privileged white people, and this is an awesome thing. But disassembled – parsing tasks and feasibility – I quickly see how my creative, social, and professional practices expect big talk from me: high visibility. In other words, as I acknowledge my privilege and vociferously dedicate myself to activating systemic changes, corrupt hegemonies ironically require me to maintain perpetual visibility. But visibility is increasingly odious to me.

My past decade's project has been to get over myself, classic middle-age. I write in my head now: no need for the page. I try to use my waking hours helping others, planning out how to forfeit a persona-based career. This mundane Catch-22 is what I spend ample time as a teacher discussing with my students. Truly. This predicament, this wellspring of anxiety, drives us in classrooms, as collaborators looking for solutions. What will we do, finally, once and for all, to sidestep patronage systems? (1) Make art about them and bitterly accept the patronage paychecks; hmmmm. (2) Rely on mutual aid and communal funding systems that are spiritually cool but not lucrative enough to pay bills, hmmmm. (3) Drop out? Hmmmm. Thankfully, no millennials or post-millennials think this "countercultural" idea is cool anymore. Isolationism has always been outmoded. Dropping out is spendy. So, what other options do we have. Minimum wage martyr? Disinterests in money transformed to poverty asceticism? Poor people never choose this route. We don't want to stay poor. In these conversations about class structures, we begin to arrive at the leveling grounds.

They ask me: *Figuring out how to live with less is key to doing whatever we want all the time?* Is it that easy. When my mentors say this, I think: *Maybe it was in the 80s, maybe it was in the 60s*. Not anymore. Students are so preoccupied with getting their feet in doors before the planet blows up that curriculums have pivoted towards describing the arts as sets of vocational skills that upon acquisition, lead to lucrative employment pathways. Which is fine, I guess. I like pragmatic talk. Roadmapping abstraction is an oversimplified concept but is essentially well-intentioned and can definitely be helpful. Particularly in class struggles, such as fights to achieve transparency in lieu of elitist and coded etiquettes. I'm happy to talk about surviving as a scrappy artist under any pedagogical rubric. Business acumen should be part of every arts curriculum.

My main goal used to be: do whatever I want, non-stop, for the rest of my life. Try not to do too much damage by existing. Wow, how that has changed. Now, I have my dream job and my dream life based on incremental daily positive actions. Yet I still battle regularly – to neurotic degrees – with how to get free. I take anti-depressants to calm this inner conflict. What am I aching to transform?

> Gnomes, the beings more closely linked to the earth, embody the desire to work with physical matter, transforming the world so that things can have a truly lasting value. They are the bastions, the yearning, the support, the heat of a household. At times their fidelity might seem stubborn, but they are always brave. (Faena, 2023)

The heat of the household. Oh, it was so easy before I decided to become a mother! Signing onto family life has so far meant buying into corrupt systems that I fundamentally abhor in order to set kid up for success. If anyone knows how to navigate family life equitably and invisibly, let me know. If someone has had the privilege to do so, I guarantee they've had support somewhere. Healing trauma is an inefficient, time-consuming labyrinth.

Watch *Beverly Hills Chihuahua*, or travel to rainforest for a leafcutter ant visit. Remember how natural laws also stipulate that elements can cojoin to build strength, stamina, and endurance? I toast my wine glass here to the miniature, the dollhouse, the radiolaria, the celebration and scholarship dedicated to anything nanoscopic, itty bitty. Are there quiet, off-grid ways to amplify and uplift? I think so. In monsterdom's interstitial abyss, possibility is our open road. We begin as a ball of cells inside a shell before morphing into fishy gilled things that exist in birdlike yolk sacs, before growing tails. Humans are totally Frankenstein's monsters: vestigial quilts of evolutionary success that patch cellular memory into our DNA. I can pretend that I'm important but truly, I'm just reconstituted material like that chair over there. I still can't fathom why colonizers feel uncomfortable with that reality.

Collaborative and often invisible forces occasionally surface, but the point is that they keep life afloat. Community, collectivity, citizenship, camaraderie are my outlooks. Students can't pass my classes without peer engagement. Dropping in for critical feedback without leaving a gift for someone else is like showing up to potluck empty handed. In emergencies, of course we can join in presence of others for uplift and nourishment, but otherwise, that effervescent atmosphere is impossible without gratitude economies. Some days, my

Cal State students are so haggard that I assign them to lay – unplugged – in the sunshine on a picnic blanket. *Is art that isn't overtly tied to social justice, environmental advocacy, etc. becoming an even more unaffordable luxury? Is free time over?* My students have been telling me that it is for a decade now, and I have resisted. Although I've started to listen since the pandemic started, I'm going to keep my flaneur flag flying.

Bubbles; earthquake tremors; diatoms; dust particles; mist droplets; sparks. The universe exists thanks to things we can't see. So much art acknowledges and marvels at this. Odes; macroscopic photography. I write this to those of us who want to do our odd things in peace, off-screen.

It's no coincidence that there so many books about "radical joy" and "pleasure activism" coming out. Deeply injected into the toxic despair that I field regularly now, among young people: pandemic, climate anxiety, inflation, can't afford to have kids, mountains of debt, what's the point? Constant suicide watch, no exaggeration. Each semester there are more of them who don't see the tangible infinite marvels everywhere, and maybe more horrifying, don't trust that ineffable marvels are even more abundant.

The only thing that seems to help people in this fragile state is telling them to make space for No Agenda. I'll just take that assignment right out of the grade book because I can. I get it: I have zero moments to spare. It took me a year and a half to get this essay made. But I remain a giant fan of spacing out and some days, can't wait to stare at the wall. "Goblin-Mode": Oxford's 2022 Word of the Year.

A gnome may become a stellar teacher, coalition builder, and cultural architect but we know from data about inequity and underrepresentation that the choice to cultivate unrecognizability remains stigmatized. I am quite surprised to get micro-aggressive, coded variants on this almost daily: *Ah, the old focus on teaching instead of publishing – too bad, all that wasted potential. – When will you write more books? – Yeah, motherhood is work but how is your art practice coming along?* I find these judgments ridiculously classist and misogynistic, like what are we really talking about, definitions of art? Then let's say that. So let me get this straight: I've worked semi-hard enough to earn the rights to cultural production and now I'm expected to crank books out for the rest of my life to prove that I'm an artist, just because it's a waste of privilege not to? Isn't that hierarchy in action. I was taught that I had the right to choose what my art is. Which is true. But I sure get flack for testing that.

Attempting functional family life, and sharing my findings, is now my art. I did not grow up in a family that held these skills, and it is a lifetime goal and honor to dig in. I am honored to have been given the opportunities to start practicing many forms of restorative justice – how to be a good community member, how to assist with land health, and how to shift from ally to accomplice to support people I admire. I'm happy to do these things without putting my name on them, like those behind-the-scenes gnomes. I wish – like everyone that I know – that support systems were in place for such lifestyle choices.

Like a gnome, I still feel that art's goal is to steer me towards joy, to be a celebratory gateway. It's easy and luxurious to disappear into what we love, it's instinctual. Makes you sick not to do it. Follow your passions, I tell my students. There's no other option. Mid-career calibrations and pivots towards generosity, it's not a new concept. Squarely in the Mother phase over here, aspiring Crone.

References

Boone, N., & Sherman, M. (2001). Designed to cure: Civil war hospitals in Vermont. *Vermont History, 69*(Winter/Spring), 173–200. https://vermonthistory.org/journal/69/vt691_204.pdf

Bousfield, J. (2022, August 11). A first-timer's guide to visiting Plitvice Lakes National Park in Croatia. *AFAR Magazine*. https://www.afar.com/magazine/visiting-plitvice-lakes-national-park-in-croatia

Branson-Potts, H. (2022, June 24). A California gold mine's toxic legacy: Inside the fight over reopening a treasure trove. *Los Angeles Times*. https://www.latimes.com/california/story/2022-06-24/fight-california-gold-mine-reopening-toxic-legacy

dreamicus. (2023). The meaning of the dream symbol: Gnome. http://dreamicus.com/gnome.html

Faena (2023). The four elemental beings of earth according to paracelsus. https://www.faena.com/aleph/the-four-elemental-beings-of-earth-according-to-paracelsus

Haraway, D. (2016, September). Tentacular thinking: Anthropocene, Capitalocene, Chthulucene. *e-flux, 75*. https://www.e-flux.com/journal/75/67125/tentacular-thinking-anthropocene-capitalocene-chthulucene/

MineWatch Coalition. (2023). Why stop the mine? CEA Foundation. https://www.minewatchnc.org/

National Park Service. (n.d.). College Hall, Vermont College. U.S. Department of the Interior. https://www.nps.gov/nr/travel/centralvermont/cv22.htm

Norberg-Schulz, C. (1979). *Genius loci: Towards a phenomenology of architecture*. Rizzoli.

Sidler, S. (2019, October 21). What is second empire architecture? *The Craftsman Blog*. https://thecraftsmanblog.com/second-empire-style/

Veness, S., & Veness, S. (2015, August 19). Where the "human fish" lurks. *BBC Travel*. https://www.bbc.com/travel/article/20150714-where-the-human-fish-lurks

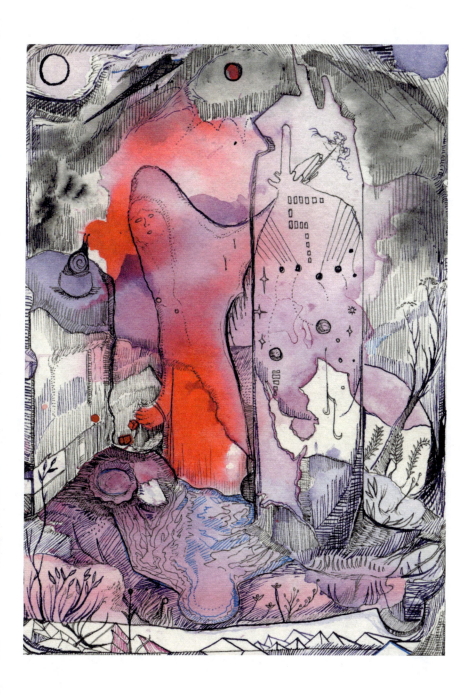

CHAPTER 5

Ghosting Ghosts

Lorenzo De Los Angeles

The ghost has had a presence throughout humankind's history as a creative force in its art, religion, stories, and folklore. As an entity that is often perceived as floating, incomplete, or transparent in form, ghosts have taught or forced us to acknowledge who, what, or once was within the physical environments in which they appear.

Humankind's fear of death may be at the heart of the fascination and willing acceptance of ghosts. This belief (though scientifically unproven) provides a certain comfort for many by supporting the concept of a life after death. A number of religions affirm this as well. People who are convinced that they have witnessed or communicated with departed loved ones will often feel gratefully reassured and protected.

However, there are also stories of ghosts that are vengeful and who seek to make known about their suffering life. A popular example found in fiction is the character of the ghost of Jacob Marley from Charles Dickens's 1843 novella, *A Christmas Carol*. Clad in chains, cash boxes, and ledger books, this ghost appears to his wealthy business partner, Ebenezer Scrooge who warns that he will also be doomed to wander in purgatory if he does not change his greedy and uncaring ways. Later in the story, three other ghosts would visit Scrooge emphasizing these points. *A Christmas Carol* is a perennial favorite which has been adapted for television and film (as of 2016, there have been 135 adaptations!) and is shown widely every year in December. Throughout my life, I cannot count how many times I have seen references to this parable that appears then disappears once a year like a phantom. My favorite version is the 1984 British-American production starring George C. Scott as Ebenezer Scrooge. Along with captivating performances and beautiful attention to period detail, it also adheres as closely as possible to the source material.

Ghosts have been popular subject matter in cinema throughout its history. Comedies such as 1984's *Ghostbusters* and 1995's *Caspar* are less common than films steeped in horror. One of my favorites in this genre is *The Changeling* made in 1980. The opening plot (no spoilers) centers on a grieving father who rents a large Victorian house to seek peace and solitude. However, it becomes apparent a disturbed ghost, that has something very important it wants to convey, has remained occupied in the house. One frightening scene involves a séance with a psychic medium using a spirit or séance trumpet, automatic writing, and a reel-to-reel recorder to establish communication with this restless entity. A contemporary example involving a similar scenario is in the highly successful horror film franchise *Paranormal Activity*, which will be releasing its seventh installment in 2022.

Before one addresses the presence of ghosts in cinema, one should go back further in time to the appearance of ghosts in still photography. Joseph Nicéphore Niépce, credited as the inventor of photography as we know it today, created the first photograph in 1826 or 1827. During the early developing process, recycled glass plates for negatives with traces of remaining emulsion would appear on subsequent photographs as ghost-like double exposures. A number of photographers soon eventually capitalized on this special effect. William H. Mumler became a celebrity by having claimed to be able to capture the faint image of President Abraham Lincoln hovering above his grieving widow, Mary Todd. Photography was a mysterious technology for many who believed that it had the magical ability to capture images of life after death. This was during an era that saw a high mortality rate due to disease, lack of effective healthcare, and major traumatic events such as the American Civil War (1861–1865).

In 1848, sisters Margaretta "Maggie," Kate, and Leah Fox heard strange sounds of mysterious origin from within the Hydesville, New York home in which they lived. They claimed to have been able to establish communication through a code of knocking sounds or rappings with a spirit whom they called Mr. Splitfoot. Word of their special abilities soon spread which led to fame, fortune, and much scrutiny onto themselves. Many imitators of the sisters soon followed, and this swiftly became the global religious movement known as Spiritualism.

Spiritualism, generally defined as a belief that communication with the dead is possible and its teachings or wisdom being useful for earthly living. At a séance, psychic mediums became the conduit between the two worlds. In this scenario, two or more people would sit at a table in a very dimly lit room. Through deep concentration, the presence of a ghost would become receptive to the psychic medium's wishes and would ideally make itself known. As was mentioned in my description of *The Changeling*, tools such a spirit trumpet (lightweight cone or horn shaped object that was said to amplify spirit voices), slates with chalk or paper and pencil (for written messages), recording devices, cameras, and sound-making instruments such as bells aided in this quest. A personal belonging of the deceased person in focus helped channel their spirit as well.

A significant device that appeared commercially in the 19th century was the talking board, spirit board, or Ouija board. The board was generally 12" × 18" in size, painted or printed with the letters of the alphabet, numbers 0–9, and the words: Yes, No, Hello, and Goodbye. Resting on its top surface was a planchette: a triangular shaped pointer with a polished underside or equipped with wheels. After lightly placing a finger onto this apparatus, it will inexplicably move to spell words or choose those on the board in response to questions asked aloud.

Use of the Ouija board became a popular pastime into the 1920s. Widespread use later faded within the next three decades (Christian religious groups, preaching that they were a harmful tool for summoning the Devil, may have led to its demise). However, in the late 1960s, the board would re-emerge along with a large interest in the occult through the hippie movement. Hippies began to gain notice in the United States of America after 1964, the year that an active draft of male soldiers for the Vietnam War began.

Angered by politics, environmental destruction, conformist social mores, racial, gender, and sexual injustices, with threats of nuclear annihilation, many people under thirty years of age began to explore non-western belief systems, cultures, and lifestyles. In this new "counterculture," older writings on mysticism, spirituality, and magic held a special appeal such as those by Helena Blavatsky, Aldous Huxley, Baba Hari Dass, Alice Bailey, and Aleister Crowley, among others.

It is worth noting in particular, that the recreational use of LSD, peyote/mescaline, and certain species of mushrooms became popular as well. The fanciful, disorienting visions imparted by these hallucinogens became manifest in concrete form through psychedelic light shows that accompanied performances by emerging bands such as Pentangle, Spirit, and the Grateful Dead. Against a blank backdrop, light show artists would create improvised, flowing compositions using film, opaque, and slide projectors combined with pulsing liquids on overhead projectors. Motorized colored gel, prism, and mirror wheels with glowing ultraviolet and flashing strobe lights, added additional colorful effects that further enhanced the altered states of consciousness of many audience members.

These multimedia productions have a historical precedent in the theatrical 18th century spectacle known as the phantasmagoria. In a dark environment such as a crypt, roving magic lanterns projected painted glass slides of ghosts, skeletons, demons, and monsters through clouds of smoke or strategically suspended fabric to create the thrilling illusion of three dimensionality. Sound effects, eerie music, tactile sensations, and suggestive, spoken narration heightened the startling, psychological effect for willing audiences.

For some, preserving the memory of the dead to further the notion or reality of the existence of ghosts has become a full time business occupation. During guided history tours, elaborate tales about hauntings in homes, restaurants, and museums help drive interest to sell tickets. This is especially true during October culminating on Halloween. Nearly 80 million Americans spend approximately $2.6 billion dollars a year on ghoulish style decorations for this holiday alone. In addition, expensive camera equipment such as indoor infrared cameras, temperature fluctuation devices, and digital sound recorders are available for professional and amateur ghost hunters or paranormal investigators. There are even a number of ghost detector or observer apps available (not for use on ghosting people) for smartphones!

Celestial and spectral forms have appeared as subject matter within my own artwork rendered by luminous, ethereal tones achieved mostly with colored pencil on paper. Pearly ectoplasm, radiant orbs, gossamer shrouds, and abstract thought-forms or auras have been a part of my visual vocabulary. I have also created a number of narrative depictions of devotional objects of death and mourning from the Victorian period. Wreaths and memorial jewelry made of human hair, postmortem and spirit photography, shadowbox shrines, mourning attire, and symbolic plant motifs as holy ghost orchids, forget-me-not, and passion flower vines, are some examples. My strong attraction to this morbid material stems mainly from three things: growing up in a Filipino-American household surrounded by devotional catholic objects (and its associated folklore), looking at my father and sister's many medical textbooks, and coming of age as a fearful yet engaged young, gay man during the AIDS epidemic (which is still ongoing) of the 1980s-1990s.

As a way of coping with ACT-UP activists' alarm of *silence equals death*, which I had equated that sex, beauty, and romance were just as deadly, I embraced the macabre, occult inspired goth subculture that flourished during that time. I listened along to the melancholic glamor of Siouxsie and the Banshees, The Sisters of Mercy, and Dead Can Dance while dressed head to toe in black clothes, corpse pale face makeup, and smudged black eyeliner, all topped with a head of wildly tangled black hair. In addition, I also delved into the 1960s counterculture and the opulent ceremonial art, magic spells, and the intricate, religious funerary practices for ensuring immortality of the ancient Egyptians.

Visual artists that have addressed the sorrow, casualties, government inaction, and homophobia caused by AIDS have greatly inspired my artwork as well. Heartrending are the nearly 50,000 handcrafted, quilted remembrance panels currently weighing in at 54 tons so far that comprise The NAMES Project AIDS Memorial Quilt, which has become the largest community art project in the world. I would also include as influential are David Wojnarowicz's uninhibited, multimedia activism, the mummy-like body sculptures of Kiki Smith, the confrontational messaging tactics of General Idea and Gran Fury, the poetic ephemerality of the installations of Felix Gonzalez-Torres, and the solemn, sculptural reliquaries of Robert Gober.

I will conclude by answering the question of have I ever witnessed a ghost. I honestly cannot say or swear with any certainty that I have, although there have been mysterious moments such as these following two in my history.

At the age of two, my family and I lived briefly in an old house located on the campus of Greystone Park Psychiatric Hospital in Morris Plains, New Jersey (my father landed his first job in the USA there as a doctor which also included on-site housing). According to family members, soon after moving into the house, loud footsteps were heard during the night. We were the only people living there at the time. After a pair of men's black shoes suddenly appeared in a closet, we soon left. Could I have had a more direct interaction with this alleged phantom then but was too young to remember? There have been a number of recorded accounts of ghosts appearing or communicating solely with young children, something possibly attributed to their greater sense or "sixth sense" of awareness, innocence, and general lack of skepticism.

In 2017, I attended a séance along with 20 other people. We sat in chairs around burning candles set on the floor and announced our names. Deep breathing meditation came next followed by calling out the spirits in the room. The psychic medium immediately stood up, walked towards me, and said that one or two very active, protective presences closely surround me. She could not identify who they might be, though out of everyone in the room, she could see and sense them most clearly. Oddly enough, random people have also approached me with a similar acknowledgement.

CHAPTER 6

Pedagogy of Necromancy

A Workshop Exercise and Its Enactment

Thom Donovan

1   **Prompt**

Like Conrad said, this shit was never a metaphor. I want to take literally the notion that the dead can do our bidding. That we can compel them to act on our behalf. Isn't that what necromancy is? What would that mean in the classroom? I don't think I've ever tried it, to be honest. But I think it would involve invocation through ritual. Who, student, do you wish to call upon to do your bidding? Perhaps it is an ancestor. A favorite author, or musician, or philosopher, or activist, or artist, or historical personage, etc. What is your wish? Is it simply for power? To save the world? Or to protect someone you love? What would you be willing to give – who would you be willing to give up (a la Zora Neale Hurston's necromancers in *Tell My Horse*) in return? Always the dues to play the blues, always the pound of flesh. How shall you communicate your wishes to command them? By intoning certain words? Through gesture? Movement? By offering food? Libation? Blood sacrifice? What are you willing to sacrifice to wield such power? Willow teleports Glory into outer space and her nose bleeds. Drew Barrymore lights a man on fire with her thoughts and her nose bleeds. In De Palma's *The Fury* Amy Irving makes John Cassavetes' head explode and her nose bleeds. Blood demands blood. What are the correct words for this reciprocity, this aneconomic debt, of spirit? What images? What sounds? What movements? How shall you prepare? Will you wear certain things? Imbibe certain foods? Stay up for long hours? Fast? How shall the dead 'mount' you? How the Lord? At the risk of becoming metaphorical, what debts are owed the dead we wish to command, and which the 'socially dead' who undergird this circle of hell? The prisoner, the detainee, the figure of starvation, of disease without cure, the refugee, the natally alienated and criminalized, the truly poor, the monstrously disfigured, the dispossessed, the abandoned, the tortured. How would you – how can you – pay your debt to them? If you have endured (social) death, what is owed you by the (socially) living? What physical manifestations of spirit? How much blood?

[Now provide a response to the questions]

2   Responses

Who, student, do you wish to call upon to do your bidding? Perhaps it is an ancestor. A favorite author, or musician, or philosopher, or activist, or artist, or historical personage, etc.

Often I call on people who I cared about now past, call them ancestors, though many are not related by blood. I call on you Grandmother, Uncle Bob, Uncle Ed, Uncle George, Aunt Kay, Aunt Dottie, Grandpa, Steve Siegel, David Nolan, the Lucys, Kevin, now Etel. Mainly, I wonder how foolish I must look on the other side of this realm; I wonder what you are doing for me already, negotiating for, if you are the reason I am alive at all. I imagine that other realm as another place – of this world and not of this world – where our fates are worked out? I don't know if I wish to command you, so much as entreat you to act on my behalf, which I realize may be closer to prayer than necromancy. I need to think more about someone I would like to call upon/command who is not an ancestor.

What is your wish? Is it simply for power? To save the world? Or to protect someone you love?

I call upon/command those I do more often than not because I wish for the world to be better, to experience less hardship and more prosperity, to thrive when everything seems precarious. Such simple wishes. Such common ones.

What would you be willing to give – who would you be willing to give up (a la Zora Neale Hurston's necromancers in Tell My Horse) *in return?*

I don't think I could ever go through with it. I could not sacrifice the people I love most, at least. What would possibly be worth sacrificing them for? How could I lose them to gain the world?

   What kind of world could I possibly want without them? Yet this is what necromancy truly revolves around. A sacrifice of something one truly loves to accomplish their task. It is impossible to imagine anything is more important than that person, including the world, including everyone else in the world. I guess that kind of makes me a monster? A narcissist at the very least.

How shall you communicate your wishes to command them? By intoning certain words? Through gesture? Movement? By offering food? Libation? Blood sacrifice?

PEDAGOGY OF NECROMANCY

What are the correct words for this reciprocity, this aneconomic debt, of spirit? What images? What sounds? What movements?

How shall you prepare? Will you wear certain things? Imbibe certain foods? Stay up for long hours? Fast? How shall the dead 'mount' you? How the Lord?

At the risk of becoming metaphorical, what debts are owed the dead we wish to command, and which the 'socially dead' who undergird this circle of hell? The prisoner, the detainee, the figure of starvation, of disease without cure, the refugee, the natally alienated and criminalized, the truly poor, the monstrously disfigured, the dispossessed, the abandoned, the tortured. How would you – how can you – pay your debt to them? If you have endured (social) death, what is owed you by the (socially) living? What physical manifestations of spirit? How much blood?

[Now compose a poem]

> Poem
> It is difficult
> Oftentimes to concern
> Myself with the
> Dead when the socially
> Dead surround us.
> It is difficult
> To consider in
> Earnest necromancy
> When the world
> Revolves around necropolitics
> (The politics of
> Death, of who
> Gets to live
> And who must
> Die). For me
> What is key
> Is the sense
> That necromancy concerns
> A balance of Forces –
> relations – and As such
> may
> Be dialectical. "Nothing

Is given for
Free," Willow says.
Might we see
The living and
The dead having A
kind of
Balance sheet, but
Also the socially
Living and the
Socially dead? ... Sounds
Return from the
Dead like a Kind
of money, A
kind of
Poetry we can
Only make with
Our blood. Poets
Have paid dearly
For their words –
That's what the
World doesn't realize.
So many debts
I owe (it
Is Thanksgiving 2021),
I know it.
So often the
Ground I stand
On doesn't
Seem to be
Mine if I
Look at it
Long enough, and
I get dizzy.
I can't believe
The shit people
Post on social
Media on Thanksgiving.
I can't believe
How many people
Wished me a Happy

Thanksgiving today. When
I close my
Eyes I see the
Dead coming back
To claim their
Debt. It's like
When those elevators
Release in *The*
Shining and blood
Splashes on the
Walls and washes
The furniture away.
I can't believe
A white man
Made that movie
(oh yes I can).

CHAPTER 7

In the Shadow of Toadstools
Fairies and the Natural World

Laura Forsberg

> Do you believe [in fairies]? ... If you believe ... clap your hands; don't let Tink die!
> BARRIE (1911, p. 197)

∴

With Tinkerbell's light flickering, Peter Pan's plea rings through the theater each night the play is performed, inviting adults and children alike to claim belief in a reality and a life beyond the day-to-day. In J. M. Barrie's 1904 play, belief is a vital life force; Tinkerbell cannot live on her own but rather lives through the fervently clapping hands of young and old audience members. In the act of clapping, each person makes the magic of Tinkerbell real.

Making the magic real is not exactly the same thing as believing in magic. Audience members, at early performances both in early 20th century London and today, rarely believe that they will walk out of the theater and encounter a fairy in the streets. What Barrie asks is that we embrace a half-believing wonder: a knowledge that the world would be deeply impoverished without Tinkerbell and her fairy kin. To clap is not to abandon an empirical understanding of the world, but rather to embrace the gaps, contradictions, and insufficiencies in our knowledge of it, viewing them as an invitation to belief – an invitation to enchantment.

Barrie's invitation to belief draws on a long tradition of representing fairies as figures of imaginative possibility. Fairies have long existed as creatures on the borders of belief and imagination, straddling the divide between real and unreal, between science and magic. Fairies ask us to consider what if: What if fairies were real? What if the crevices of nature and the shadows of toadstools contained more than we previously believed?

The existence of fairies as enchanting creatures at the margins of sight and knowledge offers a model for inviting students and colleagues into a space of imaginative indecision. Fairies, indeed, give an external from to an internal longing that exists within many of us to acknowledge and to explore the enchanting unknown all around us. Using fairies as a guide, I ask students to suspend the question of true/not true and to explore instead the possibilities contained in "what if?"

1   Fairies in the Natural World

More than three hundred years before Tinkerbell appeared onstage, William Shakespeare represented the figure of the fairy in *Romeo and Juliet* as a being who straddled nature and imagination. During the Elizabethan period and before, fairies were typically imagined as beings the size of small children, capable of mischief and mercy. Shakespeare was the first to imagine fairies instead as the minute inhabitants of the natural world. In Mercutio's famous speech, Queen Mab is a tiny figure whose diminutive body belies her power over the thoughts and dreams of all. Much of the speech is fantastic: Queen Mab sits in an empty hazelnut carriage drawn by "atomi" that gallop over the noses of sleepers and brings vivid dreams of what might – or will – be (Shakespeare, 1974, I.iv.59–63). While the speech is full of the stuff of dreams, Queen Mab is also surrounded by features of the natural world: her vehicle has wagon spokes of spider legs, a wagon cover of grasshopper wings, a harness of spider web, a whip of cricket's bone, and a gnat for a coachman (Shakespeare, 1974, I.iv.64–75). Queen Mab's fantastic nature is thus embedded within the world of natural science.

Shakespeare's alignment of fairies with both imagination and science reappeared periodically in poetry through the centuries, but it was not until the late eighteenth century that fairies began to be depicted as the miniature winged beings we know today. Thomas Stothard was the first to represent fairies with butterfly wings in his 1797 illustrations for Alexander Pope's poem *The Rape of the Lock*. According to family lore, Stothard received the idea as a suggestion from a family friend and immediately insisted that, "to be correct, I will paint the wing from the butterfly itself" (Stothard Bray, 1851, p. 32). Catching an insect in the nearby field, he proceeded to merge human and insect forms, crafting the image of the fairy that endures today. His actions, of course, raise the question: why does it matter to be "correct" to nature when you're drawing an imagined creature? Why not draw fantastical shapes purely from the mind?

Stothard's instinctual turn to the natural world reflects a broader shift. By the nineteenth century, fairyland was no longer a distant realm; it was here, in our midst. This shift was made possible by the change in fairies' imagined size; once fairies were consistently imagined as miniature beings (rather than as small, child-sized creatures), it became possible to claim that they were everyone around us – overlooked only because of their diminutive dimensions. Throughout the nineteenth century, fairy art and literature became engaged in representing the fantastic alongside the known world of nature. The children's illustrator Richard Doyle represented fairies riding carriages drawn by thoroughbred butterflies, training birds to sing, and kissing elves across toadstools. Fairy painters like John Anster Fitzgerald (known as "Fairy Fitzgerald") depicted fairies alternately at war and at peace with animals, including bats, birds, mice, and rabbits. Meanwhile, John Everett Millais painted fairy subjects from Shakespeare against a background filled with twenty separate and meticulously observed varieties of grasses. These works posed the question: is fairyland really more wondrous than the known world of nature?

In answer to this question, several authors of scientific guides for children used fairies to inspire child readers with a true sense of the wonder of the natural world. In works like A.L.O.E.'s *Fairy Know-a-bit; or a Nutmeg of Knowledge* (1868), Crona Temple's *Etta's Fairies: A Little Story for Little Folks* (1879) and Lily Martyn's *Princess and Fairy; or the Wonders of Nature* (1900), fairies guide children to an appreciation of the greater wonders of the natural world. Even as these "fairy science" books represent fairies as real, they also indicate the unimportance of fairies when compared to the greater wonders of nature. Arabella Buckley's more famous and often-reprinted *The Fairy-Land of Science* (1879) more concretely imagines fairyland not as a place but as a lens through which to view the natural world. For Buckley, all of nature is a fairyland to those who open their eyes to its enchantment and wonder.

In the first decades of the twentieth century, it was more difficult to sustain this seamless integration of science and imagination. When Frances Griffith and Elsie Wright, from 1917 to 1920, took five photographs of themselves alongside paper cutouts of fairies, they engaged an artistic and literary tradition in which nature and fancy were seamlessly represented side-by-side. But whereas earlier illustrations envisioned the merging of art and science, these images prompted a confrontation between them. Indeed, Arthur Conan Doyle published an article in *The Strand* in 1920 defending the photos from skeptics as evidence of the scientifically verifiable reality of fairies. The Cottingley fairy controversy, as it became known, brought with it a new sense that fairies posed a threat to scientific views of the world and that enchanting beliefs could not coexist with empirical science.

It is time, I believe, to challenge this assumption and to bring enchantment into the classroom and into our lives once again.

2 Fairies in the Classroom

First: a confession. I've never taught a work whose central subject is fairies in any of my classes.

Yet fairies infuse every course I teach with a sense of open-eyed wonder. They inspire me with a model of knowing that embraces indeterminacy and inexplicability.

Students are, understandably, sometimes reluctant to embrace a model of knowing that is built around uncertainty and limits. This is, I think, in part because students have experienced uncertainty in so many realms of their lives already: they know a college degree does not guarantee a job after graduation, they see governments and organizations failing to correct structural inequities, and they believe that whatever social stability currently exists could disappear at any moment in the case of another pandemic or national crisis. In the midst of this social and structural instability, it is something of a comfort to believe that the material world is fully knowable and fully known.

Fairies offer an alternative approach to knowing, in which the limits of the known inspire us to be bolder, kinder, more curious and more creative in our attitude to the world around us.

What does it look like to learn or to teach fairy belief? First, it means being open to possibilities.

This openness to possibility derives from the particular way that fairies have been imagined: as tiny beings whose existence might easily escape our notice. According to traditions, it is often children who observe while the adults around them (especially more narrow-minded scientists) remain oblivious. In May Kendall and Andrew Lang's 1885 novel *That Very Mab*, a naturalist-professor captures the titular fairy in a specimen vial while hunting for butterflies. He brings her back to his home, where his eight-year-old son instantly recognizes Mab as a fairy. The professor, by contrast, observes that "fairies were unscientific, and even unthinkable, and ... ran through all the animal kingdoms and sub-kingdoms very fast and proved quite conclusively, in a perfect cataract of polysyllables, that fairies didn't belong to any of them" (Kendall & Lang, 1885, pp. 41–42). Firm in this belief, the professor opens the vial and prepares, against the protest of his son, to impale Mab in order to examine her under his microscope; in that moment, Mab darts away. The point is not simply that the professor fails to see a fairy who is right before his eyes, but rather that he sees the entire world through a narrow lens of his beliefs and presuppositions.

Belief in fairies means keeping open the possibility that there are realities or beings beyond our present knowledge or comprehension. It means accepting, as Charles Kingsley observes in *The Water-Babies*, that the wiser men are, the less they talk about 'cannot.' That is a very rash, dangerous word, that 'cannot;' and if people use it too often, the Queen of all the Fairies ... is apt to astonish them suddenly by showing them, that though they say she cannot, yet she can, and what is more, will, whether they approve it or not. (Kingsley, 1880, p. 80)

This rejection of "cannot" allows us to consider the possibility that the world – which we often consider to be finite and knowable – is in fact replete with enchantment. It means refusing to be like the professor who denies Mab's reality based on his past learning, and instead aspiring to be like the child who sees the fairy for who she is.

For students in my literature classes, it means reading literature with a genuine openness to seeing our world in a new way. I find the genre of magical realism to be particularly productive in this regard because it unsettles our notion of what is real and uses language and imagery to represent – more keenly than the conventions of realism can – the remarkable realities of lived experience. The most magical moment in the first chapter of Gabriel García Márquez's masterpiece, *One Hundred Years of Solitude* (1970), comes when several of the characters encounter ice for the first time. This is a wonder that we all have encountered and that few of us (at least before reading the novel) have understood as wondrous.

And while the most literal form of enchantment comes in seeing the world in new ways, fairy belief also empowers us to interpret boldly and freely – to see things in works of literature that we aren't quite sure are there. Just as fairy belief is premised upon the idea that we must look closely in order to see the fairy hidden under the toadstool or behind the flower, literary analysis is built around close reading – which is the literary equivalent of gazing through a microscope. So I send my students on expeditions through literary texts looking for repeated motifs, and as they hunt for examples of birds in *Jane Eyre* (1847) or hair in *Little Women* (1868), I think of them as searching for fairies. The work of literary analysis – the labor of comparing and analyzing and making meaning – makes simple stories into magical places where meaning and beauty emerges in unexpected places.

My students are headed to a wide range of careers. They are future nurses and physical therapists, lawyers, business executives, and psychologists. The vast majority are headed for careers in which fairy belief would be dismissed as childish. And yet fairies, I believe, equip my students with the wisdom they need to succeed. Belief in fairies exists within known and accepted systems – whether of natural science or of human psychology. But believers in fairies know that our current systems are inadequate to explain all the wonders of the plant and animal world and have failed to foster justice in the social world. Believers in fairies approach the world as scientists: with the knowledge that our current systems of understanding and our current forms of social and cultural organization are provisional, in place only until we make them better. And so it is fairy believers who will transform the world, because they see beyond the world as it is to a better world – a fairyland if you will – in which nature is respected, existing authorities and structures are challenged, and the wonder of the world inspires a sense of humbleness and gratitude.

So I ask my students to clap if they believe in fairies. I ask them to listen and watch for the magic that exists in the world around us. Fairies illuminate the idea that belief is a choice that we can and do make, an affirmation that what we know is less than what we don't and that our lack of knowledge is not a flaw to be concealed, but a strength to be embraced.

References

Barrie, J. M. (1911). *Peter and Wendy*. Charles Scribner's Sons.
Kendall, M., & Lang, A. (1885). *That very Mab* (pp. 41–42). Longmans.
Kingsley, C. (1880). *The water-babies: A fairly-land tale of science* (p. 80). Macmillan and Co.
Shakespeare, W. (1974). Romeo and Juliet. In G. Blakemore Evans (Ed.), *The riverside Shakespeare*. Houghton.
Stothard Bray, A. E. K. (1851). *Life of Thomas Stothard, R. A.: With personal reminiscences* (Vol. I, p. 32). Murray.

CHAPTER 8

Witch Transmissions

Pam Grossman

Each witch's path is their own, and that is why witchcraft is both alluring and stymieing to those of us who heed its call. It is a decentralized system – "There is no Pope of witchcraft," we are fond of saying – and no single text from which our practice stems. Despite this, magical knowledge disseminates: we seek it, and it seeks us.

In many cases, learning witchcraft is intuitive. Certain books shine like beacons and we step into their beam. We follow a little-trod path in the thicket. A friend presses a deck of cards, a bundle of herbs, a curvilinear figurine into our palm and says "I think this may help." And so we listen, we look, we venture forth. And we surrender, trusting that we are entering into a relationship with Mystery. In a healthy relationship, hierarchies are fluid (if they exist at all). There is mutual guidance and potential for infinite insights – a lemniscate circuit between student and teacher. So it is with bewitched pedagogy.

Some witches are strict autodidacts and remain solitary in their practice (insofar as anyone learning from libraries, from forests, from starspeak is "solitary.") Some find a mentor or join a coven. Some choose to go through rituals of initiation, while others have knowledge passed down through family lines. No matter how a witch receives this enchanted information, there is a consistent lesson: she must meet Spirit – the ancestors, the guides, the god(desse)s – halfway, bringing not only her devotion but most significantly her commitment to action here in the material world. There is no such thing as a passive witch. Witches *do*.

My favorite book from my youth, Monica Furlong's *Wise Child*, is about a girl who is taken in by Juniper, the village witch. She teaches Wise Child the ways of plants, animal communication, astronomy, healing. At first, Wise Child is resistant to Juniper's lessons, as they require her to show up in uncomfortable ways. She must milk the cow, weed the garden, memorize challenging incantations. She learns that real witchcraft is a discipline. It requires rigor and repetition. Dirt under the nails.

Witchcraft asks the disciple to expect intellectual discomfort as well. Furlong writes, "What is difficult about learning – any kind of learning – is that you have to give up what you know already to make room for the new ideas.

Until you get used to it, it makes you feel very silly. But then the reward is that you can suddenly do new things" (1987, p. 40).

Magic is embarrassing. A belief in it – a collaboration with it – means relinquishing some measure of control, even as you paradoxically gain more agency in doing so. It means saying "I don't know how this works, but I'm doing it anyway." It means singing strange songs, speaking to invisible beings, donning sparkly garb, or casting off clothing entirely. Magic-making is inherently at odds with the status quo, even as it is one of the most consistent and most natural human practices.

For those of us who have been raised in a society built on the so-called rational, unlearning systems of capitalist valuation and metrics measurement – not to mention our own self-consciousness – is an exercise in shedding fear of judgment, rejection, persecution. Witches define value based upon what is embodied *and* disembodied and to some, this is an inherently threatening stance. We honor our sensual experiences without shame, and we find divinity within wood, blood, moon, books, and roots. At the same time, we dialog with invisible entities and put our faith in ineffable forces. We learn this by trying, and getting intriguing results. It is evidence-based yet subjective and near impossible to describe, which is what makes "proof" of witchcraft's efficacy particularly wily. And yet if it didn't work, why would we bother?

My own identity as a witch is crystalline. Every facet of this archetype – wisewoman, deviant, crone, sibyl, monstress – is an aspect of me, and as I shift into each shape, I shine. But witches also teach us that shadow is as important to honor as light, that winter has as much majesty as summer, that death is omnipresent. They fill their gardens with roses and belladonna, softness and poison. The witch is a fully-integrated enchantress, and her incantation is *everything, always, nothing, now.*

Because of this, the witch has taught me how to embrace the seemingly contradictory parts of myself and the multitude of roles I play. I'm kept supple in my thinking about my Self, because I have learned that I am in fact a bouquet of selves, I am violets and datura and snapdragons and rhododendrons and sweet pea and dandelions and vervain. I am creatrix and destroyer. I am darkness and I am every drop of light.

I am a leader and an acolyte. In the workshops and rituals I teach, my goal is not to tell my students how they should practice witchcraft. It's to show them that they can make magic with their very own signature. And so I receive the gleaming pearls of their creations and revelations, as I also take cues from Spirit – and I do my best to be a witch-bridge so that each might cross through me and find the Other. Which isn't to be falsely modest, because I also possess enough ego to believe that I have earned the right to give and to guide.

Transmuting esoterica into exoterica in support of someone else's alchemical evolution is no small feat. It takes Time. Energy. Craft.

Much has been made of the word "Craft" in relation to witch work, but it merits emphasis. For a craft is something one cultivates, and it is a somatic art. It is in and of the body. It involves hands, sweat, spit, the throat. And as such it is deeply personal. This is why artists make such excellent witches (and sometimes vice versa). Anyone can follow a recipe in a cookbook or song sheet or grimoire. And gaining aptitude in doing so requires practice and skill. But one day you may find yourself brewing your own ingredients together, singing your own melody. You may suddenly create a charm of your own devising. And it will be delicious. And it will be true. And yes, yes, yes, it will *work*.

Novalis has written, "In a work of art, chaos must shimmer through the veil of order." The same can be said for crafting a spell of any kind. A circle is cast, bones are thrown, petals are strewn, candles are lit. Incantation is invitation, and what we are welcoming is the Unknown. Maybe it's ghosts or dream beasts, deities or d(a)emons. The fact of the matter is, we can't predict who or what will arrive – we can only call out to them with splendid names. So it is with crafting a life. We prepare and beautify and hedge our bets and do our very best with what we have. And then at some point, whether we like it or not, we let go and see what happens. We hop on our broomstick, and let it take us for a ride.

And so there are many things that witches can teach us about how to be better humans. The witch helps us learn about generous generativity, the compassionate application of power, and how to best make use of one's individual gifts. She has shown me that by embracing unusual, irrational beauty one can experience true connection with even that which seems commonplace. Or perhaps more accurately: she eradicates the notion of the mundane and exposes everything and everyone as truly marvelous.

This may be what I love about witches most of all: they are autonomous agents even as they are wholly of the world(s). Like Hecate herself, the witch traverses boundaries. She is equally at home alone in a hut at the heart of a forest, swirling Sabbatically on a hilltop with her coven, or flying through the sky to have a lunar tete-a-tete. The witch is the ultimate outsider who belongs absolutely everywhere.

Reference

Furlong, M. (1987). *Wise child*. Random House, Inc.

CHAPTER 9

SMART Goals Are Magic

Amy Hale

The magician transforms and manifests. Cutting a romantic image, casting magic circles and summoning forces to bend reality to one's will, the magician, unlike the mystic, is ultimately concerned with material circumstances. Following the charge "As above, so below," for the magician, the microcosm reflects the macrocosm, earth can reflect the perfection of the heavens. The mage is in many ways an idealist, as magic reflects the clean laws of a mechanistic universe, where all things correspond to some other thing. Living in this enchanted web of correspondences, the magician crafts their vision, sets the spell, and changes the world.

My own strange 20-year journey in teaching was devoted to online learning, and then later to faculty training and finally curriculum design. Eventually I managed an instructional design department for a higher education consulting company helping faculty to develop and build online programs. Despite having left higher education for a full-time career writing about magic, I remain a true believer in the power of online education to provide access to the people who need it the most. Online learning in many ways led current educational trends toward measurement, assessment, data collection and outcomes. There were several reasons for this: One is frankly that many people simply did not trust online learning and wanted solid proof that it worked, which, when done well and properly, it does. Second, learning management systems provided data that helped us understand more about how students learn. Online learning pushed forward the art and science of teaching and has forced wider conversations about what works and what doesn't.

Over the course of my career in education I grew to love the magic of curriculum design, its elegance, sleekness and promise of transformation. When a curriculum is designed correctly and with attention to detail, each part of a course or program moves like a well-oiled machine, no moment is wasted, the instructor and the student should, ideally, be in harmony with the content, having room to explore, to be mutually changed in ways unknown and importantly ... known. Just as in contemporary magical subcultures magicians have a reputation for being stuffy, pedantic, and rigid, so do those of us who love tightly designed curricula and beautifully mapped outcomes. We are thought to kill the passion and inspirational classroom moments that many teachers and students thrive on. It is not my intention to kill those moments, it is to provide the alembic, the refining alchemical furnace where those experiences become gold.

Our magic in the classroom must be shaped by the changes we wish to effect, and so we start our spells not with the content but by refining our outcomes. So often in magical circles we hear of the unintended consequences, the way in which the magician asked for something and got much more, or much less than she had expected. Maybe the universe had something else in mind, or maybe it was actually in the nature of the request itself. The idea of crafting intentions in magical practice is a source of some debate among magicians. Some see intention as the most important part of magic and sufficient in itself, others feel they are useless without a good deal of esoteric elbow grease to slide the practitioner to success. Some feel that the act of magically stating an intention is sufficient, as words have power and they are sufficient to generate reality. On a new moon they may state aloud what they plan to do for this next lunar cycle, or they journal about what their intentions are. In some sense there is a belief that the statements themselves have a magical quality that will carry their wills forth into the unknown where their wills will be achieved. Yet seasoned magicians argue that intention is not enough. You can't create your reality simply through enchanted words, you need to back them up with real world action and with concentrated energy. This has led to competing arguments: intention is everything, intention is not everything. In reality the key to manifestation is both. Intention is critical. To get the results you want, your intention must be defined. You must follow it up with real world action but unless you have a clear map, you will not reach your destination. Teaching is the same. Your best enthusiastic classroom performance in the world will get you nowhere if your intentions are not clear. Fuzzy intentions do not ensure student success.

Aleister Crowley once called magic "the method of science, the aim of religion." Despite the romanticism of magic and the occult, magicians, certainly since the nineteenth century, have always looked for repeatable results and have often engaged with the language of science. This is why spell books and magical orders exist. There is a belief that there are right and wrong ways to do magic and that a systematic approach will be the most effective. While we know, realistically, that the results and methods of magic are not truly measurable, the desire is there. Quantifying your results is not a bad thing in either magic or teaching. Measurable is a term that makes many educators bristle, but approaches that are measurable help us to determine our success in all things magical. If we don't believe in our successes and can't say how we achieved them, are we wasting our time? Even if we choose not to reduce our results to seemingly cold statistics, graphs and charts, thinking in terms of what we want to achieve and how to accurately follow up is a useful and necessary skill.

For some teachers, crafting learning outcomes feels like an impersonal and clinical distraction from what they perceive as the real magic of teaching, the moment when they and the students sparkle with the connection of many light bulbs going on at the same time. But although those light bulbs may go on in the moment can you say for certain "This is what I set out to do with my students and I know that I was a success because so were they." The more concrete we can make our teaching strategies, the more certainty we can expect in enacting the desired and expected transformation. A well-designed curriculum is like a spell of the very best kind. We craft our intentions (outcomes) and then provide the mechanisms to work our wills (content, assessments).

There is an art to setting intentions, and while it may not seem as sexy or as mystical as letting your desires waft on the wind, mastering it will help you to tighten your vision and to get results. Be concrete. Here is where Bloom's Taxonomy is your friend. In fact, magicians of all stripes would do well to learn some Bloom's verbs, for they help shape our thinking, make it precise. Think of Bloom's verbs as the first components of your sorcery, magic words that you wield like the sharpness of a blade; compare, analyze, interpret, demonstrate. Bloom's taxonomy provides the substance for a million beautiful incantations for both teachers and mages: "I will create! I will compare! I will plan! I will design!" Weave your outcomes, your intentions, into every single thing you do in your classroom, from readings to assignments. This is how you actively and materially support your magic. Magicians could also learn a thing or two from instructional designers. Like a well-designed curriculum, magicians need scaffolding. They need to think iteratively, and know how to break down the stages of big ideas. Your spell won't be effective if you can't think in steps. All magical requests to the universe, just like the very best classroom assignments, should be SMART: Specific, Measurable, Achievable, Realistic and Time Bound.

Perhaps we can enchant the process and reception of curriculum design, to recast it from something thought of as distant and leaden, saturated with lifeless, bureaucratic malice. Let's see SMART goals as magic, Bloom's verbs as our words of power, curriculum maps as webs of correspondence linking all the elements of our classroom universe together. We can use these tools in both the online and face to face classroom to cast a magic circle for our students, to create a boundary and a space between the worlds to artfully conjure their beautiful transformation.

CHAPTER 10

The Goddess

Elizabeth Insogna

The Well, The Cave: The Earth

In the beginning all was charged with aspects of the goddess in the realm above and below. The old, old snake-bird figurines encapsulated this understanding, an understanding that allowed for an earth-dirt dweller to meet the sky with unquestioned unity. Things were connected in ways harder to imagine now. Time turned, consciousness shifted, and her command gave way to more absence than presence in the wake of monotheism. Sex and death fell to the realm of the unholy and the powers of creation were transferred from Goddess to God.[1] Turning toward The Well and The Cave we can fall through time to remember and reunite.

In my imagination The Well and The Cave contain one another. The depth and darkness in both clearly represent hidden aspects of the goddess, a magical enveloping, and a veil for transformation. Hekate's home is the cave and Demeter sits by the well whose source is flowering from the depths. Zeus whose name is connected to lightening is birthed in a cave full of light while bees swarmed at some moment in time before Jesus came back from the dead – but way after Inanna walked the depths of the earth vertically to meet the Queen of darkness, hang dead for a spell and finally suffer re-birth. The depth and moisture is vaginal – a continued connection to the black starry cosmos and to life on earth. There is a solitary, virginal quality of a space existent before trauma, rape or any other form of penetration. The Space of the Well/Cave is pure.

∴

There are many approaches to the Goddess and this essay is by no means extensive as it's a personal one that is dedicated to the archetype of The Goddess in my direct experience, spiritual contemplation, and practice according to her nature, past, present and future. She is an access portal that offers an alternate and wild approach to the organization of being especially in terms of magic and art making. My relationship to the Goddess is shaped by her ability to descend into queer space and to create an exit out of the artifice of gender construction or a conditional relationship with time.

Over the past decade I've continued to study her forms[2] and have created an especially devoted practice to the ancient Greek Goddess Hekate[3] over the past two years.[4] I harness her symbols through meditation and magical inquiry to attain a closeness that I don't fully understand but embed in my sculptures to trace our working poetic conversation.[5] I've found that this is the most direct and sincere route, since much of our knowledge concerning ancient forms of goddess is image based rather than documented in scripture. The lineage of the cult of the goddess through time, the branches of her tree in space, though often through sublimation and syncretism, help to amass ingress into her totality. Like the way quasi-crystals work – what appears to be a complex pattern is more than this – it's a never-ending mosaic that continuously recombines in time.[6] The system of the goddess is never closed or complete.

Initially, underwhelmed by her lack of presence in Judeo-Christian monotheism as well as the way monotheistic construction permeated the inside my mind and paralyzed access to the full spectrum of my spiritual being, I set out to find her. Though I grew up Protestant, the power of the virgin was lost as her agency was said to yield to the main divine entity, a vessel for the son of God, a woman as part of a larger story whose main source of light and life was a man. This was disempowering, decentering and spiritually destabilizing for half of myself.

The Greco-Roman pantheon expressed the goddess a bit better but seemed mostly dead. A slow absorption into Christianity rendered the kind of connection I needed much more difficult. This, along with the intellectual problem of the non-vaginal birth of goddesses (birthed instead from semen, sea foam and male brains[7]), I continued my search. Spending time in India in 2011, I found the Goddess, specifically The Mahavidyas, ten tantric deities of wisdom,[8] central and alive in ways that I craved deeply and hadn't found elsewhere. This has led to a life-long contemplation of their positive source of wisdom, eros, magic and inner transformation – a burning up and through.

Under the Well and Cave: The Spring, the Fire

The energy within the well is a spring – a source whose life is replenishing moisture.

The well implies verticality while the cave includes horizontality. Both reveal the unconscious mind, dream worlds; all that is occluded, hungry for light. Sex and death figure deeply while plunging down into the earth well/cave in the original resurrection myths of the ancient Greek Persephone/Kore and older still, Mesopotamian Inanna/Ishtar. In these myths the underworld is separated and ruled by another deity; the former with Hades/Dionysos, Persphone's husband, and the latter with Ereshkigal, Inanna's sister.[9] Here, the Goddess figures into cycles, a separation of worldly seasons and bridge between life and death. The Well/Cave is vaginal whose orientation is vertical and horizontal – a vertical depth of implied matrilineage and horizontal as a connector in life to life, and magical in the transmigration of this space.

The Mahavidyas whose source of worship is the Spring/Yoni is a sacred vagina in divine form and physical practice within her temples.[10] The moisture of the Spring is in full force with the inclusion of fire and water. I personally relate to their relationship to blood, sex, speech, demon-slaying and the abyss (to name a few) as metaphors for the integration of these aspects in the self on the path toward individuation. The challenges that arise in terms of meeting and integrating these details which include the taboo within the divine is a significant part of the system of the Goddess. Sex and death are present here as with Persephone and Inanna, as a totem of our liberation and an invitation to question what these meeting places are on earth. They may reveal alternate ways to relate to these spaces of transformation – and ultimately heal by allowing for our unique subtleties to come forward by coming to meet. In these living goddesses, our minds explode with possibility – a quick left-handed path to exit out of the material world, bodily fluids like menstrual blood and semen are offerings ensouled in the pure sweet abyss of the crone all in one.

The elementals of fire and water in their upward and downward movement create a cross in the spring. The notion of springing forth is mentioned often in the Chaldean Oracles with Hekate as source and world soul. The word in Greek, πηγή, is defined as both Spring and Source. The source springs forth, gushing up with a whirling movement that is fluid and fiery. In the Oracles, secrets are hidden (enfolded) in the fire of the paternal intellect whose source is Hekate. I see her libidinal space as moving along the heart which contains the boundary between the intellect and sensory. The heart is a meeting ground for spiritual accompaniment and for presence.

Hortus Conclusus

> A garden enclosed is my sister, my spouse; a garden enclosed, a fountain sealed up. (Song of Solomon 4:12)

The Hortus Conclusus, (enclosed garden) is a place carefully protected from invasion, labored over and nurtured is a place for the strange, beautiful, mundane, and divine to come together in poetic placement. I see this aspect of the

Goddess expresses herself as a pause and is a time for reflection as well as a separation from the rest of the "real" world. This separation and delay are integral to the path of individuation and self-study.

My first meeting with an enclosed garden took place in my imagination through my favorite book as a child, *The Snow Queen* by Hans Christian Anderson. In it, the main character, a girl, Greta is on a quest to find her friend, Hans. While playing together, he was struck suddenly in his eye and heart by two fragments of the devil's mirror – essentially turning both gaze and sensory input frozen – rendering him an icy eternal captive of the snow queen. Greta set out into the wild world determined to find him and bring him back to life and love. On her way she stumbles upon a beautiful walled garden. This Hortus Conclusus, created and tended to by a witch was an invitation to delay. Once inside, Greta was enfolded within the exquisite display that overwhelmed her visual cortex with hundreds of flowers in full bloom, diverse in color and species. Enraptured inside the walls of the garden, she forgot herself and intentions including her friend's name, and how she arrived there. She learned many things about the true nature of beauty, the full flame of a flower's bloom – the peak in the center of Eros: the dream before. Death and dying seemed absent in the garden, though in truth they were only buried ....

One day Greta pricked herself on a thorn from the thick stem of a rose bush, and as pain and blood broke asunder so did the awakening of her memory. Roses! Have you seen my dear friend underground with the dead? Your underground root system is connected![11] I know that you speak the language of the liminal, the bridge between worlds that contain the hidden secrets of self-creation and connected love. I know that you know the dead!

Absence and delay are needed for rejuvenation. In the dream realm a faerie like slumber sends spells over the conscious mind. Why are such spaces important? The flowers are connected to life and death, to pleasure as well as a painful re-awakening through the thorn. Sleeping in the garden of eternity before waking to walk barefoot in the dead of winter give courage – as Greta gained upon leaving The Hortus Conclusus.

Conclusion

As mentioned previously, my current focus is directed toward Hekate. When I began to work deeply with her, on a particularly long day in research and mediation, as evening fell, the presence of a black starlight filled smoke formed along my altar's edge. It looked sort of like a microcosm of the cosmos and was about a foot in diameter. The next day I vowed to study ancient Greek out of respect for her, to attain a personal closeness and greater understanding of her powers. Now, almost a year and a half later of study, I've experienced the presence again in new form – in my heart – a physical feeling of a soft flame – a light that one summer evening enveloped my whole being momentarily like a wing. The space of the intellect takes us only so far in finding the direct line to the Goddess.

Acknowledgements

Special thanks to Kay Turner (see her essay on Hekate in this book) for our conversations through the years and for directing my understanding that the Goddess is my organizational system. Special thanks to Kari Adelaide for the invitation to write on a subject so dear to me, to Karsen (Karen) Heagle for our queer kinship and understanding, and to Jesse Bransford for our friendship and connection around these ideas over many years.

Notes

1 See chapter "Hebrew God and Gender" in Ruether, 2006.
2 The long history and lineage of various goddess show connections in conceptual and iconographical ways. For example, Hekate and certain of the Mahavidyas overlap in relation to time (crossroads as an aspect of time and choice/ fate for Hekate and then Kali – literally the female aspect of time, as well as the way time moves through the various forms of the Mahavidyas, that manifest through the stages of life from youth to old age). Another example includes Hekate's multi-heads/hands and symbols: key, fire, serpents, dagger/sword, and new moon which parallel the forms and ideas found in The Mahavidyas, though this is material for a separate essay.
3 Hekate is a very old goddess. See Kay Turner's essay in this book on Hekate exclusively.
4 *Hekate's Grove* a three-person exhibition with myself, Kay Turner and Karsen (Karen) Heagle, culminates this focus, research and work for now.
5 On studies of the Chaldean Oracles from the 2nd Century AD with Hekate central to the text as the world soul, symbols come to the theurgists from her and have been said to gain in complexity if more closely related to divinities closer to earth, while reveal a minimal, formless quality by way of closeness to the Goddess/God. See *Hekate Soteira* (Johnston, 1990).
6 We are standing at one point and then another, in dreams we become other people, places even things – this ability to shift places and see another perspective, momentarily through the eyes of another is part of the work.
7 As with Aphrodite (sea foam + severed male genitals), and Athena (Zeus's forehead).
8 The Mahvidyas are ten tantric goddesses, known as a group in India since at least the tenth century CE according to some sources, though I was told directly from the Priest Rajib Sarma with whom I studied with in 2017 in Kamakaya (the main site for the Mahavidyas) that they have been worshipped for at least two thousand years. https://kamakhya.org

9. Ishtar unites with her sister physically for a moment while sitting on top of her naked, before being expelled to death, quite complicatedly giving her husband as a substitute. The Descent of Ishtar; see full text: https://sacred-texts.com/ane/ishtar.htm
10. Each of the ten temples in the Mahavidhya complex in Kamakhya, India are constructed around the original points of the spring that bubble up from the earth. The eruption of water serves as a central point of worship in each temple, the Goddess's pitha where the energies of the divine are most present. The water levels are ever changing according to the seasons. Each temple's spring is connected underground to the source. Kamakhya is significant as it's where the vagina of the goddess fell to earth when the Goddess Sati's body was ripped apart into 108 pieces with each part landing in a different part of India.
11. Another fascinating aspect of the Goddess – that which is non-visible – connective systems like root systems and streams that have the ability to interconnect quite naturally forming a hidden collective of coming together.

References

Johnston, S. I. (1990). *Hekate Soteira*. Scholar's Press.

Ruether, R. R. (2006). *Goddesses and the divine feminine*. University of California Press.

CHAPTER 11

Reflections on Alchemy

Candice Ivy

1   The Spider and the Girl

It was summertime in the deep South. The warmth of the sun and dampness in the air created a languid backdrop as two sisters played outside their grandmother's home. Resting against a supporting post, the younger sister quietly played along the wide porch. Arching and bowing around and above the child's head was a massive spider web. The spider occupying the web was enormous, almost half the size of the girl's frame. Its body was large and flat, reminiscent of an eye. This spider called herself "Anazee."

Seemingly oblivious to the spider and the web, the young sister went about her play as if nothing was out of sorts. However, the older sister could see the web spun around her sibling and beckoned for her to slowly remove herself from the web. Entranced or unaware of the lurking danger, the young girl paid her older sibling no heed. As the spider insistently crawled over the girl's now motionless body, the elder sister became fearful and panicked, determined to kill the spider so no harm would come.

Anazee quietly observed and listened to the elder sister's reactions. She thought to herself, "I will transform myself into another breed of spider so that I will not be killed." At this, she transformed into a large spindly black spider and leapt from her web towards the older girl. A battle swiftly erupted between the older sister and Anazee. Suddenly getting the upper hand, the girl stabbed the spider, but instead of dying, Anazee turned into her original spider form so the girl could see she was not dead, but merely transformed. The moment the girl recognized what had occurred, the spider abruptly disappeared.

On edge from the battle, the elder sister ventured into her grandmother's home to rest, only to discover another spider scaling the wall. Unlike Anazee, this spider was small, and non-threatening and looked as if it was a handmade wooden toy. Some of its body was painted blue, the rest was the natural color of wood. This clever spider observed the girl studying him and decided to transform himself into a man so they could speak. At first the girl was startled by the sudden transformation, but meeting her with ease, the man stood tall and possessed the familiar

© CANDICE IVY, 2024 | DOI:10.1163/9789004681507_011

sense of intimacy, like that of a lover, a teacher, or guide. He spoke to the girl in a way that suggested they knew each other well.

A long time was spent between the two, all the while the man shared stories and histories about the variety of spiders he thought the girl may encounter on her journey to come. The man specifically noted Anazee, and told of her incredible cleverness and power. "Anazee," he said, "is a queen and should not be met with uncertainty."

More than ever determined to slay this queen spider and protect her family, the girl ventured on her journey to find Anazee.

Some time passed and the girl found an unfamiliar place, but knew in her bones that it was Anazee's home. Open and expansive, the land was free of any dense forest. The earth was bare of grass, but rather covered with red clay, parched and cracked by the heat of the looming sun. People were present, but out of sight. From the subtle buzz of activity, the girl could sense their homes existed somewhere off to her right.

Behind the guise of bushes, the girl silently observed a village a short distance alongside the base of a large solitary hollow tree. Instinctively she knew she had finally found the home of Anazee.

Anazee's movements could be seen as her body passed in front of the cracks lining the great tree. She leisurely moved in and out of its large opening. Her massive body was now much larger than a human and covered with brown hair, similar to that of a rodent. The girl quietly observed as men from the village would frequently brave battle with her. Crowds would form as they attempted to kill Anazee and prove their heroism. With little effort, the great spider would crush them with weapons held in her many arms, retreating triumphantly back into her hollow tree.

Observing the tactics of the great queen, the girl decided to brave a second battle with her. Preparing herself, she cleverly began work on her armor.

Laboriously the girl hand-crafted her sword, helmet and armor out of hardwood. When finally, her weapon and armor were ready, she bravely approached the great tree. As if knowing exactly the weakness of the armor, Anazee slowly emerged from her burrow with a single weapon, a chainsaw. As the fight ensued, the girl surrendered to blow after blow to her armored arms and helmet with the chainsaw. Feeling the saw carve deep gashes into the wooden helmet and armor, the girl realized she must retreat before succumbing to her own death.

This battle left the girl shaken and weakened, but she had yet gained knowledge of how she must battle Anazee. "As every living entity has a point of weakness," she thought, "I will have to find hers." Bravery alone would not win the battle, it required patience and solitude of thought. An inner quietness had to be cultivated so the ear could be bent towards that internal guiding whisper revealing the way forward.

With this knowledge in hand, the girl quietly closed her eyes and a vision of Anazee's native home came into focus. As the vision progressed, the girl was shifted to the heart of Anazee's homeland, not physically, but within herself.

In the unfolding vision, the air was filled with bits of wood dust. The large spider began to cough through the dust irritating her lungs. At that moment, realizing that she could interact with the vision, the girl reached out her hands and collected the dust, storing it within her front pockets. The vision then revealed a large black toad with shiny oils glistening on its skin. The toad hopped within range of the spider, but in repulsion, Anazee swiftly jolted away from the creature as contact with its skin had the potential to weaken her body. Moving to pick up the toad, the girl carried it to a nearby small pond.

Emerging from the vision, the girl knew that it was time to lure the great queen to her.

Removing the dust from her pockets, the girl blew it from her hands. Caught by the wind, the dust danced through the air, in, around, and through Anazee's tree. With great agitation, Anazee moved outside her home coughing and breathing heavily. Sensing the mischief, Anazee looked up to spy the girl in the distance. With rage, the great spider lurched and swiftly scurried in her direction.

Running towards the back of a nearby pond, the girl continued to lure and beckon the queen spider.

Approaching the girl's wide and solid stance with great speed, Anazee leaped forward in her direction. With the great spider's body barreling forward through the air, the massive black toad flew from the girl's hands to make contact with Anazee's bare, exposed underbelly. The spider fell backwards hard, as if suddenly paralyzed by the skin on skin contact with the toad.

Hovering over Anazee with a large pitchfork in hand, the girl removed the toad from her weakened body and stabbed the queen thoroughly through the heart. In great agony, the spider's heart bled as she began a transformation that extended up through the pitchfork into the body and heart of the girl. At this joining, an alchemical change began to occur, merging their bodies in a sea of connection and love as they became one.

• • •

This story is from a dream I had years ago, though its wisdom continues to inform much of my life's choices as well as my artistic and teaching practice. The story is a *Hero's Journey* as much as it also embodies archetypes of the *Inner Sage* and *The Trickster as Dark Mother, or Shadow Mother*. However, the part that has resonated the strongest is the archetypal force of Alchemy. It is a shaping force that has long been a part of my life, showing up in dreams, in my artwork, and informing how I teach and navigate relationships.

From a psychological point of view, the internal Divine Alchemy is evoked when one faces primal archetypal forces strong enough to ignite your own inner well of fire. Once in contact with any archetypal force, that relationship can, if followed, result in alchemical change. It is my experience that to dance with Alchemy is to dance with many other archetypes at the same time. Alchemy is a holistic practice.

The very aspect of reading and interpreting the dream can itself be seen as an alchemical process, a merging of relationships, (the dreamer and the dreamed) to cognitively arrive at something new. For me, Alchemy is the fire that occurs out of the merging of two or more parts. The aspect of *'being in relationship'* has stood out to me as an absolute necessity for any alchemical process. Being in relationship to various parts of oneself, others and the natural world builds its own kind of heat. When two or more sets of relationships come together, a reaction will always occur. Any reaction cultivates energy, but the type of energy determines the quality of heat or transformation. In essence, energy *is* the source of all alchemical fire. One cannot exist without the other.

The conventional view of Alchemy deals with the transformation of one substance, usually a metal, into a more 'perfect' or evolved version, mainly gold. Gold was viewed as an ideal or noble metal since it did not rust or deteriorate. Before the Western world explored the notion of Alchemy, the Chinese strove to transform one substance into a cure for intractable illness, or to even prolong life to the point of immortality (Maxwell-Stuart, 2008). Through this lens, it was seen as an impetus for spiritual transformation, both for the participant and/or the alchemist themself. For more than 2000 years and across continents, various iterations of this expression have been explored.

It was believed that metals grew in the earth, like plant life, but as they grew, they would slowly, over time, transform into more perfect versions of themselves. Alchemists sought to hasten nature by activating the process of transformation through a catalyst. This catalyst was known as the metaphorical *Philosopher's Stone*, an activating and key ingredient in the transformative process. The *Philosopher's Stone*, in essence, provided the fire/energy necessary to activate change (Maxwell-Stuart, 2008).

I love the magic and mystery surrounding the idea of the *Philosopher's Stone*. In the dream, perhaps the *Philosopher's Stone* was the awareness cultivated through sensitive observation and interaction with the nemesis, Anazee. Without both, present and mindful transformation could not occur. The dream is essentially a manifestation of the psycho-spiritual evolution of transformation. However, in the outward version of the alchemical process, so many things can play the part of the philosopher's stone. Among these might be, the teacher, a class project, the creative materials, an idea or concept, and/or the relationships in one's life.

> Would you know the perfect master? It is he who understands the regulation of fire. (Thomas Norton; Hillman, 2010, p. 14)

To dance with Alchemy, one must learn to become a master tender of the fire. The art of tending the fire, and the key to alchemy means knowing how to ignite, excite, enthuse, warm, and inspire the material at hand. Materials can be physical or nonphysical: thoughts/patterns within one's own psyche or within a collective group of people, or physical materials in one's studio. Most importantly, we come to know materials, whatever form they take, through being in a *present and mindful* relationship with them.

In my artistic practice, I spend great lengths of time simply coming to know the properties of my materials: wood, clay, glass, and the ways they *may* work together. The same is true for my teaching practice. With each class, thoughtful time is spent observing and assessing subtle patterns in the group and individual students before I fully know how to shape and activate the space. Learning is a byproduct of activating and nurturing the space of Alchemy in the classroom.

A deeply personal and intimate relationship with materials, both tangible and intangible, was cultivated throughout the duration of my youth. I grew up in the deep South of the United States and in a time when the vestiges of the 'old south' still clung to the culture. Historically, my family were farmers. Being the first born grandchild in the 1970s, I was fortunate enough to intimately know my grandparents and great-grandparents. The patterns of working close to the land clung to them from their own spent youth and were passed down to me from long summers spent tilling, furrowing, digging, planting, growing and tending acres of fruits and vegetables. Then came the harvesting, canning and storing through the winter months.

Throughout my early years, I developed an attunement to natural rhythms and their ever shifting interweaving relationships. I was keenly aware of the interplay between the land, plants, animals, weather, and seasons as well as my own participation within it. This early experience provided me with an intimate relationship with material and the importance of not only observing something, but also sowing a relationship through a vivid kind of presence and interaction with those materials.

Another important factor in my long dance with the Archetype of Alchemy were youthful experiences in the Pentecostal church. Pentecostals are known for their charismatic services that often involve repetitive music, singing, chanting, leading to ecstatic altered physical states of being, known as 'holy spirit possession'. These states would sweep through the entire congregation in waves, no one was left unaffected. As a child, I noticed there were patterns involved in the cultivation and shaping of these 'ecstatic services'. They did not always occur, but over time, I began to predict when they would.

My experience in the church was both participatory as much as it was observational. From the age of six I began unintentionally falling into the collective stew of heightened energy during services. These early experiences with 'altered' states were at times revelatory and powerful, and at other times solitary and inward seeking. Over the years, I developed an understanding of subtle, somatic shifts happening within the collective during these ecstatic moments. Observation is never enough, in order to know your materials, you have to be an active participant in the relationship.

Years of experience in the church and living close to the rhythms of the land, taught me how to be both participant and witness, cultivator and cultivated, when to ignite, excite and tend and when to burn. You cannot activate and tend the fire if you don't intimately know the fire.

One final thought on Alchemy is that of union and connection. The alchemical process begets connection and ultimately a union through that connection. Lately, and from a psychological point of view, I have experienced the alchemical process of union as a kind of eros. For me, eros is the embodied space of union, it encompasses love, life and the bliss/agony of both. In the dream, as the girl pierces the heart of Anazee, the two then merge to become something new, but the embodied space of this alchemical union is love.

Perhaps this is the gold the ancient practice of Alchemy speaks to?

References

Hillman, J. (2010). *Alchemical psychology*. Spring Publications Inc.
Maxwell-Stuart, P. G. (2008). *The chemical choir: A history of alchemy*. Continuum International Publishing Group.

CHAPTER 12

Shapeshifter

Tiffany Jewell

I told myself I was a bridge.
I believed myself to be the bridge.

From one side to the other, I was the one who could connect people.
From one side to the other, I was the one who understood them all, on both sides.

I *was* both sides!

Both, Black and White.
We called it "mixed."
We called it "biracial."
I was called "other."
I was called unspeakable things.

I was THE bridge and I was just a kid.

With four braids neatly plaited and ending with brightly colored plastic barrettes, my compass rose pointed in any direction. It pointed toward every direction.
   The bridge across my little back – made of the muscle and sinew and blood and memory of my ancestors from both sides …
   From both sides.
   With the blending of those who were colonized and the colonizers.
   I thought my role was to be the bridge. I thought that was my purpose. In my childhood naivete, I was certain it was my "cosmic task."
   But then I went to school.
   There, they walked all over me and my little bridge.

∴

If I were a poem I'd be the *Bridge Poem* by Kate Rushin. 1981, we were both born. And I'd wear that poem in my hair and my eyes and in the extra melanin that helped me to blend in and set me apart, that little bit of extra melanin that helped ensure I wasn't too different and just different enough.

•••

I got tired of being tread on ... of translating ... of not knowing which kid I was supposed to be at which moment ... so I changed.

I shifted and my shape grew with me. The bridge broke, unraveled, and became almost obsolete. Shifting and changing. Transforming became easier than letting everyone trample upon me ... I could slip in and out, change who I was and fit into the scene with ease. I no longer placed myself in the middle. I stood along the sides, against the walls, and at the edges.

I didn't become aware of my own shapeshifting skills until Middle School. I knew they existed. I saw others like me on television shows and in magazines. There weren't many of us, but they were there.

I didn't get to practice before the first shift. It just happened. It was almost beyond my control. I couldn't stop it; I didn't know how. Being placed in classrooms with kids from different neighborhoods and different skin tones (even lighter than my own), school was the catalyst for my shift. And the burn of the relaxer chemicals bubbling on my scalp, the oversized flannel shirt, and the vain crushes on white boys who played the ancient game of peacemakers were proof that my bridge broke and my transformation began.

But, it always came with a cost – Exhaustion and self-loathing. Confusion and a growing absence of self. False smiles and friendships that claimed the superlative of "best", but didn't truly last.

School was where I deposited my one self for the other.

It's where I learned to, instead of translating for others, speak the language of the Valley as if it were my own. Saving my Southside accent and words for home.

School was where my transformations were completed from one day to the next.

It's where I learned to sit with the White kids at the lunch tables and lose the muscle memory of the games that were played in elementary school.

School was where I lost myself within myself and grew to be someone else.

•••

As I got older my skills became more practiced and more refined. I lost myself many times. And every time I found myself, I figured out how to hone those secret and obvious skills.

Their surprise when I would slip into my real self using my tongue to push out the truth that had been buried within. My reactions moved quicker than my rationalizations.

It's a practice, to not fall into the default of shifting, of losing yourself completely, of forgetting.

I notice the others. I see their shapes shifting. I see their backs scarred from the past. I see the power they hold and the fear of being found out. I see the ways in which Whiteness continues to be ignorantly unaware of our abilities.

I didn't need to ingest a potion. A snap of a stick of gum was enough.

It was no wonder why I loved *The Secret World of Alex Mack*.

It started with changing my appearance. My "glamour" created illusions.

My curly hair straightened.

My crooked teeth aligned.

My neck adorned with beaded flowers or a crucifix from a religion I didn't believe in.

My body dressed in baby tees and oversized overalls, in pro-reforestation shirts and tapered jeans, in long floral skirts and sweaters purchased in the women's section of JCPenney.

My locker graced with cut-out images of Jordan Catalano and Angela Chase, Michael Stipe, and Prince William.

My ears tuned to the sounds of The Cranberries's *Zombie*, Ace of Base, Buffalo Tom, and Weezer's *Undone the Sweater Song*.

I didn't need to become another animal. Nor a vampire.

I could have possibly embraced a transformation into a wer-person or a bear or a fly.

Instead, I shifted into a superhuman.

I became a different person.

I became an illusion.

Their "What are you?" was all the proof I needed that my abilities grew stronger.

Like Proteus I avoided answering their questions.

And the day I realized the school labeled me as White, gave to me so freely the very thing I had worked so hard to obtain, was the day I stopped. But the shift persists.

To blend in and assimilate, to lose myself and become a part of myself without being a whole person was something I no longer wanted to take part in. The "W" label next to my name was a violent assault on who I could be, should be, wanted to be, and was. But, school still exists.

School was where I should have been able to be me.

It could have been a place where no adult asked me to bridge one and another by asking me "Are you Black *or* White?"

It could have been a place where I could be a whole person, not just be a part or both, but me everything I was and am.

It could have been a place where my shapeshifting could have lay dormant, never to be discovered.

Because I did it to protect myself. I had to shift to protect myself and others like me.

At first, I shifted into a person I thought I was supposed to be. It felt easier than being a bridge. But, I couldn't lose myself as a bridge the way I lost myself when I transformed.

I watched myself from above and below. I listened to myself and didn't recognize who I became.

School was where I learned how to be …

I could be a model student with my good grades, peer mediator skills, and Drama Club accolades.

I could be exactly what my teachers needed me to be at any moment.

I could be exactly what my peers and classmates needed me to be.

Because I was a dream manifested by guidance counselors and school administrators.

CHAPTER 13

From the Stars or the Booming Labyrinth of the Mind

UFOs, Memories, and Myths

Alessandro Keegan

I had my first UFO sighting in 1987, when I was about seven or eight years old. It was a clear summer afternoon, and I was in a friend's backyard casually looking over the treetops at the cotton white clouds dotting a perfect blue sky. My eyes caught sight of something silver, an egg-shaped object that was moving as fast as a falling stone but with a slow, lateral rotation like a football's spiral when it is properly thrown. I told my friend to look up at the sky. Before our eyes, this spiraling silver egg passed into a wispy cloud and was never seen again.

As an artist and an art history teacher, I find the archetype of the UFO a useful description for all that is sublime and ineffable in art, all that we cannot successfully name. There are experiences unique to the artist, and to the beholder of the artwork, that slip from the grasp of communicability. As with dreams, art confronts us with great mysteries beyond the material. The mystery at the core of a work of art, the unnamable inspiration, is the true aura-rich essence that transfixes us around it. UFOs hold a similar place in our psyche. They appear as solid, technological objects, but they behave like specters and angels.

The UFO, an acronym for *unidentified flying objects* that was created by the US Air Force in 1953, has become associated in popular culture with extraterrestrial visitation and technology beyond human capabilities. In recent years, encouraged by leaked Air Force videos and a spate of mysterious objects over America's skies, US officials have taken to renaming the phenomenon UAPs, or *unidentified anomalous phenomenon*. The term I prefer remains UFO, because the UFO is more than a scientific or military designation, it is a societal force. Hurriedly emerging into our cultural landscape only a couple of years after the first atomic bomb test at the Trinity site near Alamogordo, New Mexico, in 1945, the UFOs have brought visions of divine technology into the skies above millions of observers across the world. In 1947, pilot Kenneth Arnold reported seeing unidentified flying objects over Mount Rainier in Washington State, and America's newspapers seized upon his descriptions of aerial, crescent-shaped forms that moved "like saucers skipping across the water," and the term *flying saucers* was born. That same year, there was an alleged flying saucer crash on a ranch just outside of Roswell, New Mexico, a location that is only a two-hour drive from the Trinity test site.

My boyhood UFO sighting happened at the tail-end of a long UFO flap of sightings all throughout the Hudson Valley region where I grew up. Stories of triangular configurations of lights and dark ominous masses in the sky as large as football fields had been in our local newspaper, on the nightly news, and on the popular TV show Unsolved Mysteries. This long period of consistent UFO sightings was the subject of the book, *Night Siege: The Hudson Valley UFO Sightings*, which was co-authored by Project Blue Book collaborator, Dr. J. Allen Hynek.

Whitley Strieber's book on his alien abduction experience, *Communion*, had been a bestseller in the year that I had my sighting. I was strangely attracted to the blood-chilling alien face on the book's cover, a painting by artist Ted Seth Jacobs. Every time I was at the mall I would go to the bookstore where the face of the *Communion* cover waited for me on the paperback carousel by the entrance. Eventually, I summoned the courage to read *Communion*, which was a terrible mistake. It is filled with horrifying experiences, including a violating medical examination by the aliens. It gave me nightmares. I was intrigued, however, by the dream-like, philosophical tone of Strieber's reflections on the alien abduction experience. He wrote as if his experience was more metaphysical than physical, something affecting his spirit as much as his body. "Something is here," Strieber wrote of his own experiences, "be it a message from the stars or from the booming labyrinth of the mind ... or from both" (Strieber, 1987).

At a younger age, maybe as early as four or five years old, I had had a recurring dream that paralleled some of the images described in alien abductions. I only remember this dream now because I drew pictures of it. I have a way of never forgetting anything I have drawn a picture of. This dream took place in a dark world with no walls. Scattered throughout its cavernous, shadowy expanse were what I thought of as "aquariums." These "aquariums" were made of an organic, globular metal, like frozen pillars of mercury, that were polished to a chrome-like sheen. Within these polished vessels were convex domes of glass. These orbs of glass glowed through the liquid inside them and when I peered in, I saw that dolphins were swimming within the phosphorescent liquid. There were humanoid figures as well, which I described as "frog-men," with large, dark, globular eyes on either side of their heads. I also remember that my mother and father were with me, but they were frozen, like wax statues.

In my early teens I searched my local libraries and read through every book on UFOs I could find. I read John Keel's *The Mothman Prophecies* like it was a magical grimoire, rich in Keel's mystical understanding of the interconnectedness between UFOs and other highly strange, paranormal phenomena. I began to transcribe stories and notes, coupled with newspaper clippings and photocopies, in a journal that became my private casebook on UFOs. This marbleized notebook of painstaking writing and ephemera grew over the course of two years until the book was swollen and the glued binding was beginning to separate. Beyond any religious teaching or fantasy, the UFO phenomenon was one of the most compelling and numinous myths for me as a child.

Strong myths, ones that do not explain away but rather acknowledge the mystery in all things, are incredibly influential on young children. Two centuries ago, these myths would have taken the form of fairy tales, like the stories of the Brothers Grimm. These fairy tales, rooted in pagan and animistic belief, are lighthouses in the stormy world of a child, leading them through the reality that they intuitively know is unconquerable and strange. Children are aware that grown-ups attempt to reduce mysteries to a materialist simplicity, fairytales offer children the sweetness of undiluted mystery.

The UFO is a great fairytale. It contains many *mythologems*, or the recurrent themes found in the lore of many cultures. Jacques Vallée, scientist and UFO researcher, was among the first to chart these mythologems of the UFO experience, most notably in his 1969 book, *Passport to Magonia* (Vallée, 1970). As Vallée notes in his book, certain aspects of fairy tales, myths and religious encounters are echoed by the experiences of people who see UFOs or are abducted by or contacted by the UFO occupants. The tales of visitors from other worlds, whether those worlds are outer space, fairy land, or Valhalla, have been with the human species for as long as we have been able to tell stories.

Carl Jung, the famous Swiss psychiatrist, wrote in his 1958 book *Flying Saucers: A Modern Myth of Things Seen in the Skies* that the UFO phenomenon was a projection of the mind onto something truly unknown. Jung called this process of projection *amplificatory interpretation* (Jung, 1978). This is when we confront something, in a dream for instance, so beyond our comprehension that the mind fills in our misunderstanding of what we are seeing with familiar ideas, archetypes, and possible interpretations pulled from media or religion. For Jung, the fact that the circular disks seen in the skies all over the world vaguely recalled Buddhist mandalas was in keeping with amplificatory interpretation. This does not mean that Jung believed UFOs were entirely in the mind. Jung believed whatever the true nature of the UFOs was, it was a thing beyond our ability to understand or describe. In the world of dreams, when our minds are barraged by the irrational, we involuntarily organize the information into clear, more linear stories. This also happens when we encounter things that truly disrupt reality in the waking world. Our minds attempt to construct a rational framework for these disruptions. UFO encounters, alien contacts, and abductions, can be scaffolding onto which our minds build a clearer narrative about experiences that are incommunicable.

Later in life I began to have some of my earliest visionary experiences. One experience I will describe here because it was utterly incommunicable even though it had given me an array of physical sensations, images, and meanings. It happened one summer night when I had been compelled by an unknown force to walk into the woods behind an old elementary school building. I did not walk far before being surrounded by dark trees, with no light around except the clear, starry sky.

I was compelled to climb into a thorn bush which, though it cut and scraped my skin, felt like an oddly comforting nest. I lay in this bush and looked up at the stars and then began to see schematic images form before my eyes. It was then that an unknown force manifested an image in my mind. The image was of circular realms sending signals to each other and creating smaller universes within their communications. An awareness filtered through these structures and into me. I knew that all that we were, in this world and in other worlds, were the byproducts of an ongoing communication between two entities far beyond us. A few years later I would read Plato's *The Myth of Er* and it would resonate deeply with my experience. Likewise, redolent feelings were stirred in me when I learned of the Vedic concept of "Indra's Net," which pictures the universe as an infinite web with complex, crystal worlds joining each link.

What happened that night seemed as though it were beamed into my mind from the sky above, but at the same time it was my own inner mind talking to itself. The experience, of sensing these interlocking universes, was visual, dream-like, and an indescribable feeling of having an implanted knowing. All these experiences, in particular that of an implanted knowing, or a mental "download," are common in the accounts of alien abductees and contactees, as well as the mystics of many faiths and spiritual paths throughout history. Within various frames of reference, I might have interpreted my experience as contact with aliens, gods, angels, or spirits.

I think it is best to approach these phenomena with an attitude of *unnaming*. The American psychologist, James Hillman, recommends a kind of unnaming in his 1979 book, *The Dream and the Underworld*. Dreams, for Hillman, were a language of their own, utterly alien to the daylight, defying identity, symbolism, myth, or shape. For Hillman, when confronting dreams head-on, "we must go over the bridge and let it fall behind us, and if it will not fall, then let it burn" (Hillman, 1979). I recommend unnaming encounters with UFOs as a way of removing them from their embodiment, their classification as things, so that all that might be left is the bare phenomenon. In other words, it is best to look at only what these experiences do rather than our assumptions about what they are.

This unnaming is an approach I would like to recommend for how we talk about art as well. As practitioners, teachers, or curators, we feel a pressure to define the exact parameters of an experience in terms of the daylight world, that which is materialistic and familiar. But why use this daylight language for an experience that is inherently of the night? Art is of the dream realm and that is where it needs to be appreciated. Art lives in the imaginal space where UFOs, gods, demons and spirits all dwell together as undifferentiated phenomena. The mystery of these things must not be solved for us to see them clearly, we must sit with their mystery, contemplate their twilight language, if we are to ever get near to a true understanding of how they affect us on a personal or societal level. It is a habit of us, as humans, especially academics, to try to craft names and terminology for things that are new, so that the words can be used to define what it is we are talking about. As pragmatic as naming things in the world may be, we must also be aware of the poetry and imagination that we are excluding from the conversation when we make it dogma. The names and definitions of things can be like blinders, constantly keeping the true magic of the world on the periphery.

References

Hillman, J. (1979). *The dream and the underworld.* Harper & Row.
Jung, C. G. (1978). *Flying saucers: A modern myth of things seen in the skies.* Princeton University Press.
Strieber, W. (1987). *Communion.* Avon Books.
Vallée, J. (1970). *Passport to Magonia.* Neville Spearman Ltd.

CHAPTER 14

Historical-Ish Fiction on the Legend of Baba Yaga

Jac Lahav

1   I Am Baba Yaga

Ancient hands shake as I attempt to light the skull lantern. I sense their magic is fading. What used to be an easy chore now leads to sputtering flames from the torches that line the snaking dirt walkway of cottage. It is barely a shack: mossy, rusty, and definitely not normal.

The house eagerly rises off the ground as I approach, two massive scaly chicken legs sprouting underneath it. The cracked windows let out a shrill scream, it's practically panting, welcoming me home.

This is the house of Baba Yaga

But I am not Baba Yaga.

Baba's house is a hallucination for I am in truth an artist. One who meditates too much and dreams of witches. Painting is also a type of magic; it is forgotten alchemy. My art involves three aspects: pigment, a binding medium, and a surface. Yet, the true combination of these three elements involves a fourth element, that of intention.

I spend my day weaving these three aspects together. My binding intention involves retelling misplaced narratives through colored pigments and solvents. Alone in my studio, I make these paintings on canvas while dreaming of ancient folk magic.

In my youth, I studied folk tales, hoping to grasp Baba Yaga's forgotten sorcery. My college years introduced me to the grizzled witch, with dry lectures describing her as an old woman who ate children. However, the legend of Baba Yaga has so much more to offer us. This witch was a force of nature. She embodied the rebirth of knowledge into a dark world. Baba is an elderly female Prometheus.

Covered in fiery patches of cadmium orange and ultramarine blue, I sit in my favorite painting chair, thinking about my first college lectures on Baba Yaga. How I learned about her truth, and embarked on a journey that changed everything.

2   A Terrible Illumination

"So, you want to learn about darkness?" The Professor's words formed a cloud in the gray smoke from his pipe. That first day in Advanced Folk Anthropology the swirling smoke entranced us as we sat on the edge of our seats.

The Professor stood five feet tall, old enough to be my grandfather, and hosting a barrel of wine for a belly. His wiry mustache stained yellow by nicotine dangled a pipe trailing wisps of gray smoke. The king of field anthropology, this professor was once a real life Indiana Jones. Now almost retired, he lectured to a small class of eager students.

"Where was I?" he paused dramatically, looking back up at the illuminated manuscript projected onto the wall. It showed a skinny ogress with a wrinkled old face and long spindly arms lying by her side. Her crooked nose sniffed the dark winter woods.

"Yes, yes! Baba Yaga, ogress or old woman?"

He paused again zooming into the detailed illustration. The monster held a sack that squirmed as the projector refocused. It revealed a group of sad-faced children trapped inside.

"In this story Baba Yaga steals children to cook and eat. She brings them home to her three sisters, all also called Baba Yaga in a house that continually spins on dancing bird's legs."

I yawn. The Professor's class promised to unlock the secrets of folklore, but this survey was for beginners. Where was the excitement, the adventure, the magic?

In a blink the class was over so I retreated back to the humanities library. Since my first day at university I lived amongst the smell of aging paper and leather cloth bound books, searching for any hint of Baba related tales.

Just so happens, there are *a lot* of fables of scary old women in the woods.

• • •

Grabbing a handful of volumes at the front desk I gave a soft grunt, summoning the strength of an eager academic, and descended into the dimly lit stacks.

In those musty halls, the truth about witches was revealed. I was shocked to discover that most witches didn't even fly on brooms. My Baba, for example, flew in a giant mortar and pestle, jump grinding her way across the countryside. Her pestle thumping down, causing the whole contraption to leap through the air.

Baba's culinary magic astounded me.

Her quotidian domestic uses of magic spoke to me. Holding a pestle in one hand and a broom in the other, Baba would swoop away any trail of her existence as she flew, like a mathematician erasing their work and leaving only a polished equation.

Similar tales told of Baba's detachable hands she used to accomplish both mundane and mischievous tasks. This ambidextrous Baba was described as an ancient *crone*.

The word *crone* is a curious term, it comes from the old French *charogne*. Referring to an old sheep, with deeper ties to the Latin *carrion*, or rotting flesh. This reinforced Baba allure as the companion to death.

However, these descriptions also stood in sharp contrast to the older women I knew and looked up to. The stories bore no resemblance to my ancient professors with bright silver manes and colorful scarves. They definitely weren't related to my quiet grandmother, who, at 90 years old, still walks on the beach and laughs with the moon.

History's viewfinder is not kind to older women. In one illustrated grimoire a hunched Baba Yaga travels with Death himself on the most macabre errands. The grim reaper, releasing sinful souls as the hungry Baba plucks them from the air, merrily eating freshly harvested spirits.

History's Baba was no friendly old woman.

• • •

Closing the dusty books dislodged a mist of mildew, making me release a high pitched sneeze. Echoing through the empty library halls, I realized everyone had left.

Time has no master in a library. It was night, and not only had the day passed, but the whole semester was gone in the blink of an eye.

Exiting the library to a campus covered in white fluffy snow, I reflected how The Professor had become my advisor, and winter break had arrived. Like Rip Van Winkle, I shook life into my atrophied legs and left the cold abandoned campus.

A short train ride later, I arrived home for our family's traditional Friday night supper. My mother's house was alive with an awkward assortment of extended family members. They shuffled around like sweater-laden zombies, asking the same tiresome questions like "how is school" and "what will one do with a degree in anthropology?"

The smell of my grandmother's famous fresh lentil stew and sweet bread rolls drove me mad as I set the dinner table and finally took a seat next to my dad. Our immediate family scrunched to one side of the table. My niece sat across from me, my mom next to her, and my grandmother at the head of the table. Looking upon these three generations turned the gears in my mind.

Leading the evening prayer, I watched as my grandmother lit the Friday night candles. That was when The Professor's first lecture flashed in my mind and suddenly the idea of Baba and her three sisters made sense.

The old crone archetype was a wild goose chase and my previous Baba studies were wrong! Here sat Baba and her sisters; an analogy for time and the passing of knowledge. I had spent my time searching for a magical Baba, when a folktale's true magic is an alchemical analogy.

My mind raced to the alchemical trinity of painting, its three aspects: pigment, medium, and surface. Here too there were three aspects of Baba Yaga. Her magic manifested as host, teacher, and devourer. But one crucial aspect was missing, a fourth binding principle, Baba Yaga's intention.

3   A Gentler Light

The next day I hurried back to campus, questioning everything.

Had I viewed Baba in a tainted patriarchal light? Had I fallen into the terrible stereotype of seeking a creep and off-putting old woman? The pervasive patriarchal mythos held that post-menopausal women are intrinsically bad. It claimed non-viable mothers are useless and that those who aren't objects of sexual desire must live in the woods alone. These cruel and nasty cliches poison countless witch stories, especially that of my Baba.

I desperately needed to flip the crazy crone archetype on its head.

Like my grandmother, the witch gourmand was an entry point to enlightenment. Baba's devouring her victims was only a surface threat thread that I could pull. But beyond her cannibalism were Baba's acts of service. Baba helped errant children. Baba cleaned up the countryside. Baba disposed of sinful souls. Whether necessary evils or good samaritan-ism, this was a force of *construction* not *destruction*.

Baba offers to help lost travelers while giving them wisdom or knowledge; that is, if they first complete a task. If they win, she grants a wish, but it's their failures that always grabs our attention.

I must note here the seminal Russian tale of Vasilisa, a young Cinderella character who accomplishes Baba's grueling tasks. Vasilisa is then granted safe passage home with a skull lantern to guide her.

Finally, I understood that Baba Yaga was a slavic version of Prometheus. She gives us the light to help find our way through her chaotic, dangerous, and dark world.

Like the fire she bestows, Baba is a savior, a destroyer, a mother, and often a cannibal. The escape from Baba Yaga is yet another metaphor for maternal creation, and when Baba eats her victims, she becomes an ouroboros of knowledge.

My Baba Yaga is not a person; she is a force of nature.

∙ ∙ ∙

With this new perspective, I finally proposed a thesis to The Professor. Sitting in his office, I stared at my advisor, he smelled of khaki and corduroys, waiting in silence for me to begin.

My prepared speech quickly turned to rambling under his gaze. I argued that contemporary Baba is a neutral agent of chaos. "Baba is Gaia," I proclaimed, the witch who represents nature herself, capable of neither good nor evil.

But The Professor didn't even blink.

I dove deep into Baba as an analogy of my own struggle to study. How schoolwork itself is a stand in for the chores that Baba inflicts on lost wanderers. Like young students who don't know their major yet, Baba introduces them to the fire of knowledge if they complete her impossible coursework.

Baba is at once an analogy for creative inspiration and knowledge. I argue that in order to properly use the true fire of knowledge we must train carefully in its use, lest we risk burning ourselves and those around us. Those who fail at these complex studies may end up being roasted by the same knowledge they are promised. The goal isn't always to escape Baba but to be baked and forged into something stronger.

The Professor blinked once, and so I surrounded myself with more analogies. On and on, I rambled, trying to save grace with ever-expanding tales. Baba is the guardian of the waters of life, and I would be her Ponce De Leon. Baba's chicken leg house is the first mobile home. Baba Yaga's mortar and pestle represent the daily grind of commuting ….

With that last one, The Professor had enough. He slowly grumbled and said, "I think that you … are too deep in the books."

"So much of anthropology is looking at the past," he continues, "we try to tweeze out what makes us human, but you can only get so much from ancient texts. Those who crave the true knowledge of folklore must eventually leave the library. It is time for a semester abroad."

The idea scared me, bringing up both nerves and excitement. I fumed that my ideas were rejected, yet knew deep down he was right. Real-world experience was key to my understanding.

∙ ∙ ∙

So I packed my meager belongings to begin a semester of fieldwork. But where to go? It was impossible to choose from Baba's many mythic locations.

I briefly dreamed of going to India, chasing after a Sanskrit text translating Yaga from Naga as a "serpent." Would I meet snake deities or creatures with the top half of an older woman and the bottom half a long snake-like tail?

Another option was to follow the Japanese Baba, called Yamauba or the mountain hag. This witch embodies my thesis that Baba is a spirit of nature. In the Shizuoka Prefecture, the "yamagata" comes to your house wearing only tree bark and borrows a cauldron to cook some rice. She helps lost children, feeding them lavishly for three days. It is said this Baba has fantastic detachable breasts and a mouth on the top of her head. The latter was hidden by hair and used to devour the lost children she fattened up.

The Professor put an end to my fantasies. "You are an Ashkenazi Jew! Yamauba is not your people." he scoffed. "Your people were sculpted from potatoes from deep in the woods of Poland, and that is where you will go."

He recounted to me the first written appearance of Baba Yaga in Mikhail Lomonosov 18th century grammar guide. Translating the first term was easy, and Baba came from "old woman" and the fuller term Babushka.

Yaga (often *laga* or *jaga*), however, was trickier. The Slovenian translation of Yaga meant "to anger," while in old Czech, it simply means "witch." In Serbian, *Jaga* meant to shudder in horror.

So that is what I did. I shuddered in horror and bought the most expensive one-way ticket to the old country – a land with straw-thatched wooden houses and roads of dusty clay snakes slithering through blackened ancient woods.

4   It Ends in Fire

That semester abroad was a blur. I spent the better part of three months bouncing around from small town to small town, along the forested border of Poland and Kaliningrad Oblast. Between transcribing stories from fellow travelers and eavesdropping in poorly lit taverns, I toiled on my thesis, writing thousands of words on a holistic Baba Yaga.

Throughout, I roamed the most remote black forests of Eastern Europe. My body chafed on rickety wagons as I hitchhiked along seldom-traveled ancient dirt roads.

I found nothing.

That is until one night near the end of my stay. I was about to throw in the towel and call it quits, travel back to the school with only memories of homemade pierogies. I would stay one last night, lodged at a three-bedroom inn with a steaming cup of thin dark red borscht before me.

Putting down my paperwork and craving nicotine, my feet carried me outside to smoke my second to last stale cigarette. Looking up, the remnants of a waxing moon hung in the sky. I had never seen such a sight. It was as if an ancient god with a flaming sword cut through the darkening sky and left a golden wrench in the fabric of the horizon. This was a magical night.

The crescent quickly disappeared, and as my eyes came back to earth, I saw two new bright moons staring back at me. A figure on a stump by the edge of the woods beckoned me over with the universal signal for "bum a smoke."

We spoke in a shared broken language, a mix of Polish, Russian, Yiddish, and English. This old woman with long silken gray hair looked beautiful in the night. We sat next to each other and I muddled through describing my travels, admitting my failure to find any coherent story of Baba Yaga. At the sound of that name her eyes lit up. She stood quickly, gesturing for me to follow.

In a couple of hours, we found ourselves deep in the woods. The unusual silence in this forest and the brisk cold air made time flow in a slow-meandering molasses that reminding me of those nights in the library. I finally awoke from my reverie when we got that row of torches.

...

My arm was in a vise as the harmless-looking older woman dragged me towards the flames. One by one, they lit up, human skulls lining the approach to a run-down cabin. Smelling of propane and charred meat, I expected their flames to warm the frigid cold, but these memento mori tiki torches only intensified the winter night.

I licked my cold, dry lips and glanced at the woman beside me as she nodded in approval. Her warm promise to tell me the truth of folk tales and my thirst for knowledge led me there. The moment to turn back had gone.

The cabin flickered to life in the cold firelight. My eyes began playing tricks on me, and the small hut shifted. Tilting, it began to spin ever so slowly. My eyes followed the movement and failed to notice the long white sticks beneath me. I trip and stumbled into the dark, thrusting out a hand, I barely caught myself on something hard, dry ... and scaly?

Skull lamps flared, revealing a giant chicken leg jutting out from under the house. It was both comical and surreal that this oversized leg had caught my fall.

"The house likes you!" shrieked the old woman in the darkness.

The hut rose, loomed over me as the woman laughed.

Her joy was more like a cackle, a staccato machine gun re-stating the wisdom of this visit. Perhaps it was the skull lanterns or the creepy chicken foot house, but something felt off. My host was not an innocent old babushka.

We stood there on the precipice of her house, lowering itself, inviting me into its warm quilted interior. Whichever way this night went, there was no mistake. This was the house of Baba Yaga.

• • •

Warm in Baba's house, she's brought in a bundle of sticks to prod her oversized pot-bellied stove. I sought out her knowledge, and instead found a warm hearth blessed by this comfortable silence. My eyes drank in the room's details with a ravenous thirst and one thing stood out, the flicker of that oversized stove with its unusual dancing flame.

Baba looked at me kindly as I looked at the fire. She smiled, mentioning a book I would like, and she rises to find it. My eyes followed her as I edged ever closer to the open stove door. It was warm, that dancing flame. The colors swirled like a painting with its cadmium oranges and naphthol reds.

The flickering inviting me closer, resembled something familiar, an image arising from the alchemy of light. I craned my head ever closer, leaning in. This was it. Here was the secret knowledge I sought. As the fire cackled I heard a gentle creak from behind me. Soft hands touched my back firmly, a gesture of grandmotherly love.

And gave a gentle push.

CHAPTER 15

The Hag

Metamorphosis

Ruth Lingford

The hag is a terrifying old woman. The hag overlaps the witch, but is maybe more abject, though she may have her own powers. She is sometimes shown as the source of nightmares, squatting on the chest of the sleeper and pinning them down.

She is thin, dried-up, leathery, corpse-like, a personification of ageing and death, the opposite of the sexually attractive nubile woman, but may yet be seen as sexually predatory, arousing horror in the hearts of her prey. Typically, the hag is seen as cackling and defiant in the face of the revulsion she inspires.

A few years ago, at a Somali restaurant in Harlem NYC, I ordered a drink that was on the menu, described as "a strong ginger beverage." The waiter had to be persuaded that I really wanted it, so when a cup of what looked like mud arrived, I felt honour bound to drink it all. That night I did not sleep at all but experienced vivid visions with frightening, photographic clarity. In one of these visions, I saw myself at a fork in a road. I was told that I had the choice to take the easy, downhill path and become an old lady. Or I could take the uphill path, and become a goddess. At this point a sequence of images of powerful and terrifying old-lady goddesses from around the world flashed in front of my eyes.

There are plenty to choose from – the Tantric tradition abounds in female spectres of old age and power. Chamunda, a ferocious mother goddess, for example, is depicted as a female skeleton warrior.

The Sheila-na-gig, seen in ancient carvings in Ireland and Britain, is an old woman, usually bald and often with thin, pendulous breasts, who, grinning, exposes her cavernous genitals, maybe as a warning against lust, maybe as a manifestation of the power of the female.

The Boo Hag in Black American Gullah Culture, is a kind of old-lady vampire who obtains sustenance from squatting over their sleeping victim and sucking their breath, leaving them exhausted. They may also steal their skin.

The Cailleach in Gaelic mythology is the hag-goddess of the weather, especially storms.

The figure of the hag may be seen as the remnant of pre-Christian goddess-worship, maybe made abject to disempower her threats to the dominant religion.

In this interpretation, she is surely related to figures such as the terrifying Coatlicue, Aztec Mother Goddess, represented wearing a necklace made of human hearts, hands and skulls. The famous statue of Coatlicue was excavated in Mexico City in 1790, but was soon buried again, as the power of the image made the colonisers fear that she could ignite a new resurgence in the ancient religion. The Aztecs also gave us Itxpapaloti, the obsidian butterfly, a skeletal figure with jaguar claws.

In the parts of Africa where the voodoo religion is dominant, a post-menopausal woman gains social status and power, while in many other parts of Africa, old age may be enough to get a woman accused of witchcraft.

In Western society, the hag may manifest in the shape of the "battle-axe" a powerful but highly derogative term for an older woman who gets things done, and also the mother-in-law figure, a mainstay of humour for many centuries.

In the 16th Century, the sin of envy was depicted as a malevolent hag with pendulous breasts, often eating her own heart. According to Deanna Petherbridge, the malevolence of witches was due to their envy of fertility.

The hag may represent the universal fear of ageing and death, projected onto the woman.

Rubens and Caravaggio pair the seductresses Delilah and Salome with their hag-mothers, the resemblance between them showing us the passage of time and the evil and horror under the surface of the beautiful woman. They stand as a form of visual mother-in-law joke, though the terror underlying the joke is manifest.

A famous optical trick asks the viewer's perception to choose between the beautiful young woman and the ugly hag – they are both present in the same picture but cannot be seen at once.

The hag reminds us of the inexorable passage of time, and the inevitability of death, and she challenges us to look change and death in the face.

The hag often has the power to transform herself, sometimes, as in Scandinavian lore, into an animal, sometimes into a beautiful young woman, as in the case of the hag-wife.

One of the most famous, and most terrifying transformations in our culture is the scene in Disney's *Snow White*, where the queen brews a potion and transforms herself into a terrifying hag. The transformation from nubile woman to hag recurs in animated film, and helps us see the hag for what she is – a creature possessed of terrifying power, especially threatening to the masculine principle.

Tex Avery's *Red Hot Riding Hood* shows a lustful wolf in a scenario where the nubile Red Riding Hood is replaced by her grandmother, a sprightly and sexually aggressive character. The prospect of sex with this post-menopausal woman is so horrific that the wolf chooses the option of jumping through the window of a skyscraper penthouse rather than acquiesce to her advances. Interestingly, a version (Red Riding Hoodlum) where the wolf marries Grandma and has half-human half-wolf children, was censored.

Joanna Quinn's telling of the Wife of Bath's Tale, from the s4c/BBC's *Canterbury Tales* Series, contains an exquisitely rendered hag character (Quinn used her grandmother's body as reference) and minutely examines the transitions between young and beautiful and old and sexually repellent.

Disney's *Sword in the Stone* 1963 contains a sequence where Madam Mim demonstrates how she can turn from hideous to beautiful and back again.

In *The Witches*, Angelika Huston's sexual (though rather Masculine) persona is transformed into the hideous hag that makes her evil visible.

As a teacher of animation, it is the transformative, metamorphic quality of the hag that is most compelling to me.

Metamorphosis is, arguably, animation's special power. Our eyes are convinced of seamless transformations between objects, states and emotions. Opposites become united, meanings elided. These changes have a quality akin to poetry, where concepts can collide to form new meanings. The animator, who must effect these changes in laborious increments, comes to understand the process of change. Metamorphosis seems to me to be by its nature subversive and revolutionary, allowing us to imagine change in even the immutable circumstances of our lives.

Generally speaking, an animator approaches a transformation sequence by finding a mid-point between the two points. This may involve a poetic colliding of the two qualities, may go through a distinct intermediate shape or may, like the transformation inside a pupa, involve the breaking down of form into an inchoate state before rebuilding itself in a new form.

The mid-point is a state which contains both ends of the process, but is neither. And each step on the way along the transformation is inherently unstable, in the process of change.

For my students, the process of animation teaches them that they cannot will something into being with thought alone, but creation must be mediated through the body, with its intrinsic fallibility and tendency to make mistakes. The hand has its own logic. The repetitious nature of animation drawing is somewhere where the unconscious can take over the hand, nudging the image into surprising and revealing changes.

This familiarity with the tiny unstable increments of change is one that has a parallel for me in the process of ageing – the inexorable but magical transformation for me and half the human race from nubile woman to hag. Every morning's first look in the mirror is a frame of animation on the way to the hag.

My experience of ageing shows me that to be an old woman is to choose between being invisible and being frightening. Between being an old dear or a battle-axe. A sweet old lady or a fearful goddess.

Incidentally, the Somali drink turned out to have been phenomenally strong coffee ... I had in effect spent the night viewing my dreams in a state of full alertness.

Reference

Amiras, M. (2021). *Snow White and the seven signs of menopause: The magic mirror—A cautionary tale from the elders*. Academia.edu.

CHAPTER 16

Where Is the Lie

Anansi the Trickster, Traveler, NFT*-Minter*

Maria Pinto

Anansi bookmarked the page that this moment is written on with a thick plait of silk and is scanning it with his many eyes, laughing. The laugh is a high titter – it bounces to and fro from millennium to century. Orlando Jones, actor, is Anansi, *fired from the pantheon*, which makes the laugh ring higher, fired from *American Gods*, perhaps because he played a stirring rage too black in a slave ship's hold, so blackly stirring the clip went viral and viral and viral again on his web. Black in its rage and blackly sardonic and black in its wink. All eight of Anansi's eyes are shining like wet onyx as he laughs and are his eyes wet with anger or mirth or are they simply glinting hard, reflecting on the slyness of his next trick? But is he laughing with us or at us? Is he for *us* or against *us*? We sit in the discomfort of not knowing, on a Sunday night in America, the color from our screens dancing in our eyes. His character won't last – brother Nancy stirred the Africans to kill the whiteness at the helm to please him and that would never do, has never done, shall never do, or shall it. Who is us, the ones stirred on a Sunday night on couches and beds in basements? Who is America? That discomfort we're sitting in, of not knowing, is where the story, every American story, is spun.

    I asked everyone present in my grandmother's living room in Jamaica over the winter holidays if they remembered any Anansi stories. My nurse mother, tailor uncle, and teacher aunt all said yes, but when pressed found it difficult to elaborate. I said I would check in about it later. I am annoying, I know, these things come together only when I fail to let them drop. When I asked my mother again, over text, she sent along two links – one to an 18-year-old article about Anansi tricking his way onto a transport to a cricket match and another to a Jamaican travel site with a story about Anansi outsmarting a snake. These links had the whiff of pacification, so I asked my mother point blank, "Are these stories you *remember* remember, or are you basically like 'Here, let me google that for you?'" To which she replied, "The latter." Later still, I asked my aunt, a retired officer of Jamaica's education ministry, what she remembers of Anansi stories either over the course of her career or as they might whisper to her from early memory. She said that she didn't really recall anything from youth – she wouldn't have been focusing on that sort of thing – but that the 4th-grade language textbook had a story in it ... something about Anansi and a cow. My mother, hearing our conversation conducted over a videocall, chimed in that she only had a vague recollection of those stories being "in the air." Being told, perhaps, around a game of dominos with rum flowing or in the streets as the older kids kicked up red clay dust on their way home from the other schools. The stories made them laugh – they weren't that serious – they weren't meant to be processed as lessons. (There is a different strain of Anansi story that sounds more like one of Aesop's fables and I think it's safe to say they're everyone's least favorite variety).

My family knew the broad strokes, that Anansi outsmarted other animals much further "up" the food chain than he, and he did so repeatedly, without fail. A predator far from the apex but able to keep himself from being predated upon. I find it eerily beautiful that those I've asked can name this power while not recalling any of the specifics of any one narrative. What better way to school than to do so lightly, to make your influence indistinguishable from the air? If the tales can let a decolonizing body feel its power to navigate a colonizer's dubious morality, they've done the work.

Is it necessary to be able to tell an Anansi story or should you leave the telling to him, in the form of your black life, the one that you almost always only survive by bending the rules? It might be enough to know you know these stories.

I wonder if Anansi was there in 8th grade, ready to suggest a novel exit strategy when I ran afoul of the Burney twins (fraternal, jheri-curl-dripping, both big-eyed and lovely in my memory). They heard I'd called them ugly and sent an emissary to challenge me to a fight. Despite appearances, my knees like tennis balls in otherwise empty stockings and my razor-sharp elbows, I *could* fight, I was learning a martial art at the time. But the punishment our sensei doled out for fighting outside of a sanctioned spar was to spend the entirety of the next class running laps around the perimeter of the dojo. I was not eager to suffer such a sentence, having watched and snickered as my hothead classmate did it, meeting after meeting. The twins would not have known how keen I was to avoid that, so when they bore down on me in our apartment complex, gathering a crowd eager to witness my pummeling, they would have read it as unhinged cowardice when I sat down in the middle of the street on a speedbump in the lotus position, singing under my breath. Cars backed up, and the situation grew too chaotic for them to comfortably rain down blows on my one head with their four fists. They retreated in disgust, promising to catch me unawares next time.

As a trickster he is collapsible, totable, storable, many-faced and many-accented, able to shrink back and lay in wait. Our Anansi is a traveling storyteller.

He came with us in our oversized duct-taped boxes and trunks and battered suitcases and thatched plastic bags.

I imagine that traveling Anansi also stayed on the continent, closer to home. Was Anansi laughing when the Congolese Plantation Workers Art League (CATPC) minted a non-fungible token of a sculpture made by their ancestors to contain the spirit of a Belgian rapist colonizer, Maximilien Balot, who was killed during a 1931 uprising? In the 1970s, the sculpture was sold away from the community that made it to an American, but more recently, the artist's collective asked to borrow the sculpture of the colonial officer from the Virginia Museum of Fine Art, where it had ended up. The museum said it would eventually hand it over but dragged its proverbial feet, lending it out to other Western institutions in the meantime. I wonder if tears of laughter are rolling down Anansi's cheeks when he hears the museum director call the CATPC "unprofessional" for using images from the VMFA's website to mint and sell the NFT?

The name of the game is pleasing himself. There are stories in which he never appears personally, but which nevertheless bear his eight-footed print. And I know them when I hear them, because they echo with his laughter.

CHAPTER 17

Sibyl Pedagogy//Civic Pedagogy

Kris N. Racaniello

> The Sibyl, with frenzied mouth uttering mirthless words, unadorned and unperfumed, reaches to a thousand years with her voice by aid of the god[s].
>
> HERACLITUS, 6th century BCE[1]

∵

Prototypically, the epithet "sibyl" conjures shadowy images of women as frenzied, intoxicated mystics or prophetesses. Sibyls were oracles of ancient Greece and Egypt. Broadly, they shaped the sociocultural landscape of the ancient Mediterranean and Southwest Asia. These were women who lived on the grounds of special, sacred sites, forming an integral part of institutional religion. They created divinatory prophecies used by politicians and local leaders when making civic decisions. In essence, they acted as mystical guides in difficult times. The historical sibyl was the fundamental point of contact between religion and politics in the ancient world. She was the connection between civic, political, and religious life through her prediction's ability to change the course of secular actions.

Though there were many ancient Greek sibyls, the oracle at Delphi is the only one explicitly associated with spirit-possession (Stoneman, 2011a, p. 1). It is from this sibyl that the impression of the "frenzied mouth" and uncontrollable prophecy derives. Fundamentally, this sibyl's knowledge is not her own, but delivered through her mouth by a consuming spirit – at Delphi, that spirit was the god Apollo. Losing her sense of *self* was the key to her prophetic vision. Sometimes presented as a riddle, or otherwise formatted in obscure language, the sibyl's prophecies were word-puzzles with no definitive shape. Instead, she revealed the future through her audience's interpretation of the phrases she uttered. Many ancient stories "especially in Herodotus" revolve around the drama ensuing from an incorrect interpretation of these oracles (Stoneman, 2011a, p. 1).

Oracles and sacrifice were twin pillars of Greek civic religion. In theory, these elements of civic ritual evaporated with the abolition of all Pagan observances by the Christian Roman Emperor Theodosius I in 395 CE, but this is far from true (Stoneman, 2011b, p. 26). Oracles continued, sometimes attached to Jewish, Christian, or Muslim shrines. Presence, possession, and prediction took center stage in debates over *imago* and iconoclasm.[2] Desire to unlock 'primordial' knowledge led to the consultation of dream books or sacred texts believed to be of ancient origin throughout the medieval and Modern periods across most societies and cultures. Divination in many forms – from tarot to tealeaves to forecasting the weather – continues today. Many of these forms of divination draw on the archetype of the sibyl, transforming these Greco-Egyptian women into signifiers of hysterical prophetic vision, fortunetelling, and foreboding omens.

Archetypes do not consider the lived experience of these bygone women's lives; their fears, fortunes, worries, and triumphs. An archetype carries a shadowy figment – an idea's cultural impression – through history. Even by the time of the Roman Empire, the sibyls of ancient Greece retained only a whisper of humanity, viewed as mystical goddess-priestesses, they became signifiers of Rome's unique investment in its Greek cultural heritage. In ancient Rome, socio-political problems were deferred to the religious sphere through the collegiate interpretation of the *Sibylline Books*, an act performed by fifteen men known as the *quindecimviri sacris faciundis* (Sarlota, 2008). These were a compilation of oracular statements supposedly purchased from a sibyl by the legendary last king of Rome, Lucius Tarquinius Superbus. The cult around the *Sibylline Books* was integrated into Roman society and functioned as an interpretive manual for the public religious observances deemed necessary to avert unusual disasters like comets, earthquakes, showers of stones, plague, and so forth. The *Books* were not used for exact predictions of definite future events but functioned as an opportunity for the *quindecimviri* to redirect public anxiety and assert their elite control of public action through interpreting the oracles and proscribing rites of expiation. The public never saw or read the oracles themselves, creating fertile ground for corruption and abuse. Sibyls dwindled to an archival whisper.

The sibyl-as-archetype continued beyond Pagan ancient Rome through medieval Jewish and Christian traditions with the compilation of the *Sibylline Oracles* (not to be confused with the ancient Roman collection we just discussed, the *Sibylline Books*). Drawing on the useful blueprint created by the *Sibylline Books*, the *Oracles* folded in apocalyptic proclamations that seemed to foreshadow events in the Book of Revelation (Collins, 1984). Beyond theology, the ancient Sibyls have continually inspired many great works of fiction, including Virgil's *Aeneid* and Dante's *Inferno*. Dante drew heavily on Book six of Virgil's *Aeneid* when he composed the *Inferno* (Spiegel, 1998). In Book six Aeneas is guided to and through the Underworld by a sibyl named Deiphobë, whereas in the *Inferno*, the author Virgil himself becomes the guide, replacing and simultaneously echoing the role of the sibyl. Alluring and mystical, the sibyl archetype has acted as a sounding board for alternative thought, production, and creativity for thousands of years.

Forming a blurry archetype, the sibyl lives in my personal, pre-teen memories. Early encounters with the prototypical ecstatic sibyl occurred in my middle and high school classes. Riverhead's public school offered three languages for instruction: French, Spanish, and Latin. My childhood obsession with the occult, mythology and popular "dirtbag" medievalism naturally led me to take Latin, a course taught in middle school by Lorene Custer and in high school by her husband Dr. ("Doc") Jeff Greenberger. Fridays were designated "mythos" day, a day devoted to the study of Latin myth and culture rather than grammar exercises and memorization. On one mythos day we discussed the sibyl. In my recollection, she was presented as a feminist mytho-historical figure. I was intoxicated by the idea of this sibyl and I retained my fascination with this archetypical, powerful woman even to the present day.

In 2007 the movie *300* aired in theatres and our Latin class, somewhat miraculously, convinced the school administration to designate "cinema" as a valid field trip. In the movie the oracular sibyl is controlled by the Spartan ephor, the five hooded men described as "inbred swine" by the movie narrator. Historically, the ephor were elected officials and extremely dedicated to the city and civic life. However, this masculinity-fetish-flick presents the hooded ephor as pedophile rapists who control the naked, youthful sibyl with misty, aerosol drugs invoking satanic panic-like iconography.[3] In *300*, the sibyl was stripped of agency and victimized. Inverting my feminist hero, I saw a mirror of this manipulated, abused, and agency-less sibyl archetype in another sibyl: *Sybil*.

In a hot, sweaty high school classroom my psychology 101 class watched the 1976 movie *Sybil* the following year, 2008. The year before, a made-for-TV remake aired, renewing interest in the original. The film focused on the relationship between Multiple Personality Disorder (MPD) – now known as Dissociative Identity Disorder (DID – and child abuse. Dissociative Identity Disorder (DID), according to the National Alliance on Mental Illness, is

> characterized by alternating between multiple identities. A person may feel like one or more voices are trying to take control in their head ... People with DID will experience gaps in memory ... Women are more likely to be diagnosed, as they more frequently present with acute dissociative symptoms. (National Alliance on Mental Illness, 2022)

The powerful performance in *Sybil* linked this image of fractured identity and dissociation with trauma and a loss of agency – a physical loss of control over the identity of "self."

At sixteen, the movie stuck with me, further butchering my admiration for the powerful vision of the ancient sibyl as an oracle reaching across gendered and ethnic inequalities to affect civic change. *Sybil* was the ultimate vision of the ecstatic mystic, brought into the present day through clinical diagnosis. No longer possessed by Apollo, the Sybil/sibyl was a fractured victim possessed by trauma. As a character, Sybil's frenzied secrets were interior revelations that, rather than affect civic change, crippled the protagonist with her own past.

Rather than promote a positive, productive union with the sacred and the self, the image of the Sybil constructed within a moral-panic-plagued United States was fractured and weak. On closer examination of the history of this archetype however, the sibyl emerges as an emissary of open, intuitive, interpretive pedagogical engagement within the spectrum of her feminist and misogynist cultural manifestations. Her divinatory powers draw on a dissolution of her own ego coupled with receptive, automatic, and somatic productions. Her body is a vehicle for memory and foresight, her mouth, capable of uttering the unutterable. Her vision is unbiased by disciplinary boundaries, traditions or even by adherence to dominant grammatical structures. The sibyl reveals that meaning is created through interpretation and context.

The Delphic sibyl has been an especially potent primary archetype. A frenzied, spirit-possessed mystical oracle, the sibyl at Delphi allowed her sense of self to decay and merge with a secondary being. Representative of both empath and incoherent utterances, the Delphic sibyl moves beyond normative modes of comprehension. She is beyond the self and beyond predictable thought. She affirms interpretation producing meaning, but also looks beyond standard disciplinary language to intuitive fabulation. From this archetypical figure, we might expand our pedagogical practices to include creative fabulation. To validate student exploration and include discourse communities that are normally exiled from our fields actively validates the long historical archetype of the sibyl as a pedagogical methodology.

Sibyl/Sybil affirms the potency of knowledge production beyond dominant power structures and constraints. For these archetypes, disability and possession are tools transmitting un-utterable secrets. Whether intoxicated, abused, and incoherent, or lyrical, ecstatic, and mystical the ancient sibyl kept the secrets of the gods, society, and leaders. They muttered them for interpretation and moved things and people without ever moving themselves. Creatively expanding normative discourse beyond comprehensible rules, the sibyl represents a unique opportunity to envision a method of teaching that moves beyond normative interpretive discourse, expanding our notion of civic boundaries and interpretive communities. The archetype offers the benefits of creative production from a position that decenters the self and discursive expectation. Sibyl reveals her own secrets and keeps them, too.

Notes

1. See Malay, 2010, p. 4. This is the oldest reference to the sibyl, appearing in Plutarch's *Moralia* wherein he quotes the words of Heraclitus noted above.
2. Generally, on this debate see Kessler, 2007.
3. The "satanic panic" is a moral panic, a phenomenon wherein a society experiences a popular, nearly viral panic fearing moral threat from a particular group or idea. The bibliography on this subject is extensive, but for recent and engaging study see Hughes (2017) and Frankfurter (2003).

References

Collins, J. J. (1984). The sibylline oracles. In J. Collins (Ed.), *The literature of the Jewish people in the period of the second temple and the Talmud, Volume 2: Jewish writings of the second temple period* (pp. 357–381). Brill.

Frankfurter, D. (2003). The satanic ritual abuse panic as religious-studies data. *Numen*, *50*(1), 108–117.

Hughes, S. (2017). American monsters: Tabloid media and the satanic panic, 1970–2000. *Journal of American Studies*, *51*(3), 691–719.

Kessler, H. L. (2007). *Neither god nor man: Words, images, and the medieval anxiety about art, volume 29*. Rombach Verlag.

Malay, J. L. (2010). Sibylline heritage: From ethe mists of antiquity. In J. Malay (Ed.), *Prophecy and sibylline imagery in the Renaissance: Shakespeare's sibyls*. Routledge.

National Alliance on Mental Illness. (2022). *Dissociative disorders*. NAMI.org.

Spiegel, D. (1998). *The Aeneid and the inferno: Social evolution* [Graduate Paper], MIT.

Stoneman, R. (2011a). Introduction. In R. Stoneman (Ed.), *The ancient oracles: Making the gods speak* (pp. 1–4). Yale University Press.

Stoneman, R. (2011b). Possession or policy: The case of Delphi. In R. Stoneman (Ed.), *The ancient oracles: Making the gods speak* (pp. 26–39). Yale University Press.

Takács, S. A. (2008). The making of Rome. In S. A. Takács (Ed.), *Vestal Virgins, Sibyls, and Matrons* (pp. 60–79). University of Texas Press.

CHAPTER 18

Traversing the Boundaries of Fairyland

Kari Adelaide Razdow

In the realm of fairyland in fantasy literature and folklore, themes of unlearning hold court, and what is known is prone to unravel and reconstitute as something unknown: rules, rhythms, and assumptions are continuously upended. Fairyland elevates acts of perpetual and purposeful wandering; and, at times, becomes a space that human protagonists may detect, enter, and be changed by. Fairies themselves are not emphasized for the way they learn rites, but instead are assumed to inhabit a space that is fully vested with magic and magical powers. The fairy archetype portrays far flung and freewheeling examples of knowledge acquisition and transmission. Human engagement with the fairies pre-supposes and presents magical outcomes, while also retaining arcane modes of locating the fairy realm that, in itself, is reminiscent of circuitous pursuits of knowledge and art making.

Stories about fairies or elves are summarized by J. R. R. Tolkien in *Tree and Leaf*. As Tolkien reflects on fairyland's terrain and the denizens therein, he uses the term "Faerie" to identify a realm that deals with states of enchantment:

> Stories about Fairy, that is Faerie, the realm or state in which fairies have their being. Faerie contains many things besides elves and fays, and besides dwarfs, witches, trolls, giants, or dragons: it holds the seas, the sun, the moon, the sky; and the earth, and things that are in it: tree and bird, water and stone, wine and bread, and ourselves, mortal men, when we are enchanted. (1953, p. 9)

This realm of enchantment includes not just nature spirits or phantasmic dwellers of elfland, rarely glimpsed, but also our very selves when under a state of enchantment. Fairyland is a desirous and fleeting domain that at times may be sensed or experienced, but eventually fades with consequences that frequently careen with time itself. Often, crossing the boundaries of fairyland leads to mutations of the passage of time (accelerated, slowed down, paused, or altogether halted), and for the emboldened fairyland drifter, perils loom large.

Fairyland, elfland, and the lore associated with such realms frequently involve an arsenal of puzzling rules and vexing courses of action, mostly nonsensical, weird, and non sequitur. These rules often deal with ritually interacting with the natural world, accompanied by anecdotes and imaginative explanations used to describe or decode nature and natural forces. Some of these tenets include methods of protection against fairies and prescribed actions to gain beneficent favors, blessings, and magical gifts – including knowledge and skill-sets, practical and creative alike. In fairyland, enchantment deals with illusion, glamour, and trickery aligned with the transmission of material gifts from fairies, as objects in fairyland tend to lose their appearance or structure once carried outside of its borders.

The Scottish folklorist Lewis Spence sheds light on fairy as a term and theme, examining the rich origins, lore, customs, stories, and root of the term fairy:

> The great majority of those writers who have faithfully examined the origin of the word 'fairy' are of opinion that it was distantly derived from the Latin noun fatum, or 'fate', that is the word which describes those goddesses, the Fatae, who were supposed to govern the trend of human affairs, and who are also known in Latin by the name Parcae, and to the ancient Greeks as Moirai. Some authorities believe that the Latin word fatum gave rise to the Italian fata, and, through Roman provincial influence in Spain, to the term hada; and that in later Roman Gaul it also took the form fata. There, in accordance with a law of Celtic phonetics, the 't' was slurred, or elided, which gave it the sound of 'fa'a', and in the plural 'fa'ae.' This, later, in early French, came to be pronounced as fa'ee, and still later as fee, from which again came the English 'fay', almost certainly the product of Norman-French influence. (1948, p. 114)

The somewhat traceable origin of the word fairy does not encompass the ephemeral origin of fairy stories themselves – these taproots are complex, and Tolkien's following reflection acknowledges uncertainty surrounding this inquiry:

> What are the origins of 'fairy-stories'? That must, of course, mean: the origin or origins of the fairy elements. To ask what is the origin of stories (however qualified) is to ask what is the origin of language and of the mind. (1953, p. 17)

Tolkien also reflects on the timelessness and constant revisions and retellings of fairy-stories:

> Speaking of the history of stories and especially of fairy-stories we may say that the Pot of Soup, the Cauldron of Story, has always been boiling,

> and to it have continually been added new bits, dainty and undainty. (1953, p. 27)

The folklorist Katharine Briggs sheds light on how this aspect of storytelling takes on archetypal dimensions as lingering beliefs are potentially reworked and passed on:

> The famous pronouncement of Friar Bacon's Brazen head – 'Time is, Time was, Time is past' – might well be taken to apply to English fairy beliefs. ... The strange thing is that rare, tenuous and fragile as it is, the tradition is still there, and lingers on from generation to generation substantially unchanged. Every now and then poets and writers draw on the tradition, and make out of it something suitable to the spirits of their age. Sometimes this passes back into tradition, and perhaps alters it a little, it may be less than the critics and folklorists contend. (1967, pp. 3–4)

The archetypal quality of fairy beliefs being passed on, but slightly altered in the light of the present day, enables investigations of pedagogical themes as they continuously emerge in art and storytelling.

1 Encounters of Fairyland's Boundaries

Although fairyland may be considered at large as a realm dealing with enchantment, it is worth investigating depictions of how one may stumble or attempt to deliberately come upon this space, let alone enter it. There are rules involved, and the process of examining folklore alongside works of fiction sheds light on the patterns and illustrations of arriving at fairyland after first astutely sensing its boundaries. To begin, there isn't a sense of control one may execute when encountering fairyland, and Tolkien describes how a "crossing of the ways" is wholly dependent upon chance:

> Most good 'fairy-stories' are about the *adventures* of men in the Perilous Realm or upon its shadowy marshes. Naturally so; for if elves are true, and really exist independently of our tales about them, then this also is certainly true: elves are not primarily concerned with us, nor we with them. Our fates are sundered, and our paths seldom meet. Even upon the borders of Faerie we encounter them only at some chance crossing of the ways. (1953, pp. 9–10)

Control and deliberation are abandoned to prioritize chance. Despite perils and shadows, a fairy encounter is possible. The process of encountering fairyland requires delicate and wondrous circumstances, and Tolkien furthermore reflects on how this realm evokes wonder while revealing hardly any information:

> I propose to speak about fairy-stories, though I am aware that it is a rash adventure. Faerie is a perilous land, and in it are pitfalls for the unwary and dungeons for the overbold. And overbold I may be accounted, for though I have been a lover of fairy-stories since I learned to read, and have at times thought about them, I have not studied them professionally. I have been hardly more than a wandering explorer (or trespasser) in the land, full of wonder but not of information. The realm of fairy-story is wide and deep and high and filled with many things: all manners of beasts and birds are found there; shoreless seas and stars uncounted; beauty that is an enchantment, and an ever-present peril; both joy and sorrow as sharp as swords. In that realm a man may, perhaps, count himself fortunate to have wandered, but its very richness and strangeness tie the tongue of a traveler who would report them. And while he is there it is dangerous for him to ask too many questions, lest the gates should be shut and the keys be lost. (1953, p. 3)

The phrase, "the land, full of wonder but not of information" implies that within the realm of fairyland, curiosity is not quenched by conclusive answers, and universal emotions or feelings abound with little dependence on particularities: stars are uncounted.

Wandering to fairyland does not pave the way for comprehension in terms of retaining facts; furthermore, fishing for answers is framed as unwise and potentially perilous. There is a puzzling predicament of how one may exude curiosity without crystallizing questions, while deliberately adopting an active sense of wonder. Curiosity has no closure, in fairyland. At times, logic unravels or is altogether disavowed. Relinquishing oneself to the flow of experience and remaining open and curious overrides impulses and expectations of seeking answers. Fairyland at times also involves an avoidance of recording or communicating experience, as Tolkien describes, "richness and strangeness tie the tongue of a traveler" (1953, p. 3). In fairyland, one privately accepts experiences, however quirky or strange, and these experiences are oftentimes intensely internal, as one casts deep attention onto the natural world to attain heightened reflection and become transported.

This sentiment of embracing the quizzical and relinquishing oneself to wonder in fairyland is depicted in George MacDonald's work of fantasy literature, *Phantastes*:

> It is no use trying to account for things in Fairy Land; and one who travels there soon learns to forget the very idea of doing so, and takes everything as it comes, like a child, who, being in a chronic condition of wonder, is surprised at nothing. (1970, p. 24)

Fairyland encourages acts of unlearning to greet newness and bow to the quest of wandering and becoming. In fairyland, wonder is enmeshed with intensity, and enchantment involves losing oneself:

> I was in Fairy Land, where one does very much as he pleases ... I seemed to lose myself in the great flow of sky above me, unbroken in its infinitude ... Why are all reflections lovelier than what we call the reality? ... Yea, the reflecting ocean itself, reflected in the mirror, has a wondrousness about its waters that somewhat vanishes when I turn towards itself. All mirrors are magic mirrors. (1970, pp. 75–76)

The intention of understanding things in fairyland is no use, and rather the voyager is carried to a space that encourages a labyrinthine sense of being lost, as certainty is side-lined. This acceptance of fleeting elements and the abandonment of systematic inquiries have pedagogical tenets that induce imagination, openness, and wonder. Fairyland elevates experiences that are not easily grasped, understood, or communicated. Comprehension can be faint or loose and the fairyland traveller is owed nothing as far as the transmission of knowledge goes. Fairyland entails enclosures of strange perfection that can be accessed and traversed, but sometimes at a steep cost as enchantment eventually and inevitably fades.

Cast adrift from preconceived notions, one may attempt to negotiate occurrences within fairyland although it is *no use* trying, due to enchantment: "all mirrors are magic mirrors." The closest proximity to an examination of the reality of fairyland is to heed its boundaries of flux. The idea of openly accommodating wandering without being gobsmacked by uncertainty disrupts the shackles of the routine. Furthermore, traversing a realm that is accessed only by chance – charged by and with wonder – invokes a strange momentum that carries wanderers to new and unfamiliar territories, through magic mirrors, across reflective waters, and beneath unbroken skies, where surely strange music can be heard.

2 Fairyland Wanderings and Strange Perfection in George MacDonald's *Phantastes*

The trope of timelessness and the notion of subverting time and space are quite common in the genre of fantastic literature, but in fairyland these themes are especially central. For example, we see time flashing by, unmeasured and fleeting, in *Phantastes*:

> The time passed by unheeded, for my thoughts were busy. ... for I had no means of measuring time; and when I looked back, there was such a discrepancy between the decisions of my imagination and my judgment, as to the length of time that had passed, that I was bewildered, and gave up all attempts to arrive at any conclusion on the point. (1970, p. 140)

Judgement is placed on the back burner and measurement is skewed, inconclusive, and eventually abandoned. Rosemary Jackson reflects on the topsy-turvy and distorted tenets of time in fantasy literature:

> Classical unities of space, time and character are threatened with dissolution in fantastic texts. Perspectives and three-dimensionality no longer hold as ground rules: parameters of the field of vision tend towards indeterminacy. (1981, p. 46)

With the rules of so-called reality up in the air, including space and time, anything seems possible, and actuality versus appearances must be grappled with. The protagonist in *Phantastes* revels in the strangeness of fairyland, albeit with hesitancy:

> You see ... Fairy Land is full of oddities and all sorts of incredibly ridiculous things, which a man is compelled to meet and treat as real existences, although all the time he feels foolish for doing so. (1970, p. 197)

Although potentially absurd, encountering fairyland involves wildly accepting "incredibly ridiculous things," and G. K. Chesterton writes, "If I have drunk of the fairies' drink it is but just I should drink by the fairies' rules" (2004, p. 73). And what are the fairies' rules? Italo Calvino illuminates how "the pleasure of fantasy lies in the unraveling of a logic with rules or points of departure or solutions that keep some surprises up their sleeves" (2004, p. 134). In *Nameless Things and Thingless Names*, Lance Olsen muses upon the relationship between the fantastic and postmodern consciousness;

Our preconceptions of what constitutes the impossible are assaulted every day. In other words, postmodern art faces the problem of responding to a situation that is, literally, fantastic. No wonder, then, that fantasy becomes the vehicle for the postmodern consciousness. The fantastic becomes the realism our culture understands. (1987, p. 14)

A sense of understanding, in the realm of the fantastic, often entails not just wonder but of stepping back and confronting the unknown, unshaped, unformed, and unresolved. Yet, the powers of nature are whole and vast. Often, fairyland is teeming with flowers, birds, mosses, and insects, showcasing an ephemeral stagecraft of the earth, as seen in *Phantastes*:

> I forgot I was in Fairy Land, and seemed to be walking in a perfect night of our own old nursing earth. Great stems rose about me, uplifting a thick multitudinous roof above me of branches, and twigs, and leaves, – the bird and insect world uplifted over mine, with its own landscapes, its own thickets, and paths, and glades, and dwellings; its own bird-ways and insect-delights. (1970, pp. 44–45)

This glamour of the earth is adorned with "its own" ways, its own whirring perfection, its own delights, and its own strangeness. In *Phantastes*, we are granted only glimpses of this zone, without clarity or accounts for the passage of time:

> I will not attempt to describe the environs, save by saying, that all the pleasures to be found in the most varied and artistic arrangement of wood and river, lawn and wild forest, garden and shrubbery, rocky hill and luxurious vale; in living creatures wild and tame; in gorgeous birds, scattered fountains, little streams, and reedy lakes, – all were here. (1970, pp. 82–83)

The environs of *Phantastes* are only partly described, allowing one's imagination to fill in the unspoken elements. The above passage suggests that only a half effort – although not half-hearted – may be summoned in attempting to repaint fairyland in the afterword of experience: "I will not attempt to describe the environs." Furthermore, reflections beyond the fleeting moments do not necessarily chase the comet trail of one's experience in fairyland: "One story I will try to reproduce. But, alas! It is like trying to reconstruct a forest out of broken branches and withered leaves. ... I cannot tell" (1970, p. 95). Despite the impossibility of full recall, nostalgia may rear its head, given fairyland's strange perfection that seems impossible to replicate: "everything was just as it should be." Narrative reconstruction is collaged by mystery and eclipsed by a tenuous sense of time: "I can attempt no consecutive account of my wanderings and adventures" (1970, p. 65).

In Ursula K. Le Guin's essay, From *Elfland to Poughkeepsie*, a different sense of gravity, solitude, and purpose prevails when taking on mysterious and private journeys to fairyland:

> Elfland is what Lord Dunsany called the place. It is also known as Middle Earth, and Prydain, and the Forest of Broceliande, and Once Upon a Time; and by many other names. Let us consider Elfland a great national park, a vast and beautiful place where a person goes by himself, on foot, to get in touch with reality in a special, private, profound fashion. But what happens when it is considered merely as a place to 'get away to'? … A great many people want to go there, without knowing what it is they're really looking for, driven by a vague hunger for something real. … But the point is that you are not at home there. It's not Poughkeepsie. It's different. (2004, pp. 144–145)

Le Guin illuminates how elfland or fairyland is known by many names, and she considers it as a place that involves a heightened selfhood as one is propelled along by "a vague hunger." She describes it as both private and profound, framing it as a destination where one earnestly ventures in solitude, without a preconceived aim in mind except to extraordinarily "get in touch with reality," somewhere away and unfamiliar.

Tolkien describes this type of desire as "The magic of Faerie":

> The magic of Faerie is not an end in itself, its virtue is in its operations: among these are the satisfaction of certain primordial human desires. One of these desires is to survey the depths of space and time. Another is (as will be seen) to hold communion with other living things. (1953, p. 13)

Tolkien suggests that "primordial human desires" may be quenched in this realm, but nonetheless there's that looming question of how one accesses elfland or fairyland in the first place, to "hold communion with other living things." Accessing this domain is hardly straightforward, but we are given hints of passage.

3 Encountering Boundaries of Fairyland in Lord Dunsany's *The King of Elfland's Daughter*

In *The King of Elfland's Daughter*, Lord Dunsany describes where "Elfland touches Earth as far as poet has sung" (1999, p. 90). This convergence itself is rich, and the boundary of elfland harnesses desire, even though detecting it is elusive. Traversing the boundaries fairyland necessitates the idea of going forth and continuing on a journey, even if the destination is incomprehensible or impossibly distant, while keeping a strong hold on belief in a quest in order to detect, identify, and eventually cross boundaries to transcend the everyday:

> The beautiful boundary of twilight had drawn his desires towards Elfland, next moment his hounds had turned him another way: it is hard for any of us to avoid the grip of external things. (1999, p. 144)

In *The King of Elfland's Daughter*, the boundary of fairyland is the muse, endlessly chased and sought after, set apart and beyond, caught and lost in a series of occurrences:

> So Alveric strode on through the luminous air of that land whose glimpses dimly remembered are inspirations here. And at once he felt less lonely. For there is a barrier in the fields we know, drawn sharply between men and all other life. (1999, p. 15)

Once stepping beyond this barrier, fairyland provides a passageway where meaning clings to mystery. The dim recollection of what lies beyond "the fields we know" vanquishes loneliness, replacing it with inspiration.

While recollection may be compromised, a half-understanding may be attained, albeit with clinging barnacles of strangeness:

> There was perhaps less mystery here than on our side of the boundary of twilight; for nothing lurked or seemed to lurk behind great boles of oak, as in certain lights and seasons things may lurk in the fields we know; no strangeness hid on the far side of ridges; nothing haunted deep woods; whatever might possibly lurk was clearly there to be seen, whatever strangeness might be was spread in full sight of the traveler, whatever might haunt deep woods lived there in the open day. And, so strong lay the enchantment deep over all that land, that not only did beasts and men guess each other's meanings well, but there seemed to be an understanding even, that reached from men to trees and from trees to men. (1999, p. 15)

Apprehension is entangled with enchantment, and enchantment is spread "deep over all that land." *Guessing* meaning equates to *an understanding*, and the above passage also sheds light on a profound connection to nature: "an understanding ... that reached from men to trees and from trees to men." Clarity lurks in the trees and acceptance is reached despite "whatever strangeness" presents itself in full sight, not hidden away or haunting but at last revealed, with its mystery temporarily thwarted. In *The King of Elfland's Daughter*, there's no clear method or roadmap for a traveler to find elfland. As far as finding fairyland or elfland goes, enigma reigns strong, and there is no north star to follow:

> Was Elfland a mystery too great to be troubled by human voices? ... Or might a word said of the magical land bring it nearer, to make fantastic and elvish the fields we know? To all these ponderings of Alveric there was no answer. (1999, p. 89)

Nonetheless, there are some hints of a passageway to elfland, more mythopoeic than practical in terms of specific methods. No crystalline path is set out for the wanderer, but hope helps: "All men knew that to seek for Elfland one needed a strong hope, and without it one saw no gleam of the Elfin Mountains, serene with unchanging blue" (1999, p. 107).

Even though traversing the boundaries of fairyland seems tenuous in *The King of Elfland's Daughter*, there is a suggestion of a gravitational pull towards the realm that is inspired by desire, hope, and curiosity:

> Go forth ... and pass the fields we know, till you see the lands that clearly pertain to faery; and cross their boundary, which is made of twilight, and come to that palace that is only told of in song. (1999, p. 2)

Elfland therefore presents a quest to go beyond "the fields we know":

> Go then with your face turned towards that light that beats from fairyland, and that faintly illumines the dusk between sunset and early stars, and this shall guide you till you come to the frontier and have passed the fields we know. (1999, p. 3)

This quest involves self-enchantment and perpetual speculations of fairyland's nearness, as well as a celebration of not the destination but of a detection of "the border":

> Just as thorn trees all lean away from the sea, so toadstools and every plant that has any touch of mystery, such as foxgloves, mulleins and certain kinds of orchids, when growing anywhere near it, all lean towards Elfland. By this one may know before one has heard a murmur of waves, or before one has guessed an influence of magical things, that one comes, as the case may be, to the sea or the border of Elfland. (1999, pp. 66–67)

The act of arriving at fairyland is like guessing an influence, such as perceiving a particular slant of a wildflower: "by this one may know." One is expected to earnestly turn attention inward, in solitude, as well as cast an eye towards the natural world to perceive, watch, and listen to landscape. The *idea* of arriving propels a traveler forward, even more so than the act of arriving, even if the border is impossibly hidden and typically inaccessible. In *The King of Elfland's Daughter*, the point of access to elfland is depicted as a marsh, where boundaries are unfixed and in a constant state of flux, given the shift of water and land:

> And soon he was come by unsure paths to the reeds and the thin rushes, to which a wind was telling tales that have no meaning to man, long histories of bleakness and ancient legends of rain; while on the high darkening land far off behind him he saw lights begin to blink where the houses were ... for the marsh ran right into Elfland. Between him and the nebulous border that divides Earth from Elfland there was no man whatever, and yet the traveler walked on as one that has a grave errand. With every venerable step that he took bright mosses shook and the marsh seemed about to engulf him. (1999, pp. 201–202)

This passage depicts elfland as an enclosure that has an engulfing pull that is irresistible, even though it exudes the enchantment of "tales that have no meaning to man." Perhaps meaning is not owed to any fairyland wanderer.

The borders of a marsh are nebulous and there are no portals or classical gates for entry, only "venerable steps" towards the destination. This path is taken in solitude, without guidance or direction, and there's a sense of being honorific towards nature and relinquishing oneself to the flow of experience. This flow of experience resists being natural, but it is not necessarily unnatural or imaginary; rather, there's a state of enchantment at play. This enchantment extends to the passage of time:

> I have said that no time passed at all in Elfland. Yet the happening of events is in itself a manifestation of time, and no event can occur unless time passes. Now it is thus with time in Elfland: in the eternal beauty that dreams in that honied air nothing stirs or fades or dies, nothing seeks its happiness in movement of change or a new thing, but has its ecstasy in the perpetual contemplation of all the beauty that has ever been, and which always glows over those enchanted lawns as intense as when first created by incantation or song. Yet if the energies of the wizard's mind arose to meet a new thing, then that power that had laid its calm upon Elfland and held back time troubled the calm awhile, and time for

awhile shook Elfland. Cast anything into a deep pool from a land strange to it, where some great fish dreams, and green weeds dream, and heavy colours dream, and light sleeps; the great fish stirs, the colours shift and change, the green weeds tremble, the light wakes, a myriad things know slow movement and change; and soon the whole pool is still again. It was the same when Alveric passed through the border of twilight and right through the enchanted wood, and the King was troubled and moved, and all Elfland trembled. (1999, p. 40)

This depiction of elfland suggests permanence of "eternal beauty" and stillness that is immune to interruption: nothing stirs, fades or dies and there is an intensity of changelessness. In fact, change makes elfland shudder and during a rare instance of stirring, the borders are porous, allowing for passage. However, this entry is only temporary: "He soon discovered, as sooner or later many a man must, that he had lost Elfland" (1999, p. 70). The consequence of this temporary access involves undergoing the accelerated passage of time upon one's return: "Quite ten years must have passed away during that one blue day he had spent in Elfland" (1999, p. 27).

This consequence involving the accelerated passage of time is a common theme associated with fairyland encounters, as depicted in folklore, described by Spence:

> One of the most pregnant and interesting phases in the folk-lore of Fairyland is associated with the belief which lays it down that the passage of time in the elfin world moves at a different tempo from that known to our own sphere, that time in that mysterious region is for some reason greatly accelerated, in the view of mortals at least, and that human intruders who have penetrated to it find on their release that what seems a night has actually occupied a year of human time, or, in certain instances, a generation. (1948, p. 303)

Given this predicament of time passing at an accelerated state, the amount of time with a fairy encounter is typically quite short, as described by Briggs:

> Encounters with the fairies are almost necessarily brief, for under ordinary circumstances men are supposed to see them only between one blink of the eye and the next. In old times children were often exhorted not to fix their eyes because this was taken as an attempt to see the fairies, or at least a condition in which they might be seen; and such sights were thought to be dangerous. (1967, p. 155)

Even casting one's eyes on fairies momentarily is considered an encounter that may have grave consequences, according to Spence: "To see, or to speak to fairies was in some cases regarded as unlucky or even fatal" (1948, p. 195).

Despite potential perils, Spence's research reveals there are some rituals that may lead the way:

> The process of laying the head on the knee was therefore a recognized ritual by which it was believed one could at least trace the path to Fairyland, and bespell one into an enchanted slumber. (1948, p. 160)

An enchanted slumber may also be influenced by or induced by location: "Adults were often carried off if they chanced to sleep on a fairy mound" (1948, p. 256). Aside from chance, Spence provides another example of a ritual leading to intentional entrance:

> In some parts of Scotland the manner of entering the round grassy eminences known as fairy hills was by circling one of these nine times 'towards the left hand', when a door would open and the mortal investigator would be admitted to the subterranean abode of the fays. (1948, p. 277)

Upon embarking on this admission, though, safeguards should be in place:

> If a person found himself in a fairy dwelling he should stick a piece of steel, a knife or needle or fish-hook, in the door, then the underground denizens would be unable to close it until he went out again. ... guidance to Faerie was granted by a ball or apple which rolled automatically before one. (1948, p. 277)

This concept of what one should or should not do as a safeguard against the fairies sometimes involves uttering a saying, or avoiding certain words altogether:

> When speaking of the fairies one should always mention the day of the week ... no mention of fairies should be made on Mondays and Thursdays. If you do mention them on those days, you should say: 'My back to them and my face from them.' (1948, p. 311)

Feigning ignorance of fairies, if breaking rules, is considered a protective measure. There are other rules that apply to certain days of the week: "In the Highlands, it was thought sinister to speak of fairies on a Friday nor must their colour of green be worn on that day" (Spence, 1948, p. 311).

Another rule involving clothing mandates turning one's clothes inside out to avoid the peril of encountering fairy folks:

> An old English rhyme runs: Turn your cloakes,/For fairy folks/Are in old okes. One way of avoiding fairies in old England was to turn one's coat or some other garment, inside out. (Spence, 1948, p. 20)

At times, these rules may seem nonsensical, and lyrically weightless, such as turning a jacket insight out, or putting oatmeal in one's pockets, or following a curiously rolling apple. Sometimes these rules involve windless concerns about winds themselves:

> The fairy eddy or whirlwind can scarcely be considered without reference to the Sluagh, these traditions arising from a common source. Those eddies of wind which arise suddenly, sometimes even in the calmest weather, were formerly believed to be the media for fairy flights, and it was thought that mortals were frequently borne off in them by the elves. In order to avoid being caught up in them, people would cast earth from a mole-hill, a knife, a bonnet or a shoe at the eddy, in order to compel the fairies to restore their prey. ... If a knife be thrown, it is thought that it will wound the elfin riders on the whirlwind. (Spence, 1948, p. 64)

Dealing with fairies does not involve trying to dominate or control nature, but there are negotiations and engagements, however strange, such as indeterminately tossing an object in the wind. Spence identifies that "a certain formula for securing any person or object which the elves may be bearing off" is saying or chanting "mine is yours and yours is mine" (1948, p. 258).

There's a sense of ritual that involves being honorific toward nature, while being swept along in a flow of experience to give witness to mystery and magic within the natural world. Fairyland seems to be a place where you need to be giving and on guard, and this realm may give back to you. There is a discourse or conversation with nature that seems nonsensical but also honorific and asks the participant to do away with predispositions (for example, turning one's jacket inside out or throwing an object at an invisible target).

The acquisition of magic in fairyland re-engages its practitioners with a lost vision of humankind's relationship with the environment, granting reverence to nonhuman beings, plants and animals, insects, nature spirits, and whimsical modes of existence, while rejecting control and logical analysis. The fairy archetype subverts the idea of learning and instead welcomes ambiguity and acts of unlearning, accommodating a flow of experience that is open-ended and less dependent on time. Furthermore, the fairy archetype engages with shifting boundaries, as opposed to perceiving clear cut dimensions of things, and learning outcomes are elusive and unmoored.

4 The Transmission of Knowledge in Fairyland in Patrick Rothfuss' *The Wise Man's Fear*

In Patrick Rothfuss' *The Wise Man's Fear*, the protagonist, Kvothe, is drawn to fairyland following the lure of a song which leads to a sensation of detecting and succumbing to the pull of magic: "There was magic here, real magic" (2011, p. 700). Once arriving in the realm of fairyland, the process of learning magic from a fairy is far from straightforward:

> "I was wondering," I said carefully, "if you would be willing to teach me." She reached out to touch the side of my face gently. ... "Have not I already begun?" ... I realized that she did not intend to teach me magic. Or if she did, it was magic of a different kind. (2011, pp. 723–724)

Kvothe's questions are pitched to the fairy with caution and some frustration, without expectations of clarity:

> I asked Felurian a few careful questions about magic, not wanting to offend her by prying at her secrets. Unfortunately, her answers were not particularly enlightening. Her magic came as naturally as breathing. I might as well have asked a farmer how seeds sprouted. When her answers weren't hopelessly nonchalant, they were puzzlingly cryptic. Still, I continued to ask, and she answered as best she could. And occasionally I felt a small spark of understanding. (2011, p. 725)

This depiction of a "small spark of understanding" seems to give a nod to the limit of learning in fairyland, no matter how many questions are presented:

> After a handful of questions ... I quickly learned it was better to follow along, quiet and confused, rather than try to winkle out every detail. ... You might think these thousand facts gave me some insight into the Fae. That I somehow fit them together like puzzle pieces and discovered the true shape of things. A thousand facts is quite a lot, after all. ... But no. A thousand seems like a lot, but there are more stars than in the sky, and they make neither a map nor a mural. (2011, p. 727)

The concept of learning something, however small, is sufficient, but this feat of comprehension co-exists alongside lingering confusion:

> After our shadow-gathering expedition, I asked more pointed questions about Felurian's magic. Most of her answers continued to be hopelessly matter-of-fact. How do you take hold of a shadow? She motioned with one hand, as if reaching for a piece of fruit. That was how, apparently. Other answers were nearly incomprehensible, filled with Fae words I didn't understand. When she tried to describe those terms, our conversations became hopeless rhetorical tangles. ... Still, I learned a few scraps. What she was doing with the shadow was called grammerie. When I asked, she said it was 'the art of making things be.' This was distinct from glamourie, which was 'the art of making things seem.' I also learned that there aren't directions of the usual sort in the Fae. Your trifoil compass is useless as a tin codpiece there. North does not exist. And when the sky is endless twilight, you cannot watch the sun rise in the east. (2011, p. 738)

Kvothe experiences a complete sense of disconnect between teaching and learning as it relates to outcomes full of "hopeless rhetorical tangles."

Learning involves a continual process of negotiation: "Still, I learned a few scraps." And what can be learned may not be retained, since memory is perhaps compromised in fairyland:

> I have a good memory. That, perhaps more than anything else, sits in the center of what I am. It is the talent upon which so many of my other skills depend. I can only guess how I came by my memory. My early stage training, perhaps. ... Wherever it came from, my memory has always served me well. Sometimes it works much better than I'd like. That said, my memory is strangely patchy when I think of my time in the Fae. My conversations with Felurian are clear as glass. Her lessons may as well be written on my skin. ... But other things I cannot bring to mind at all. (2011, p. 739)

This fogginess goes hand in hand with the experience of traversing fairyland and recollection may be patchy and far from lucid.

Most often, the depictions of fairies bestowing or granting knowledge and skill upon individuals does not entail a process of learning by practice, study, or trial and error. The gift of being taught charms and skills are often conferred through magic, instantaneously. Examples of these transmissions are plentiful in folklore:

> Skill in various crafts is often a gift of the fairies. The chief of them is the gift of music. Finger Lock, a tale about the McCrimmon family collected by Hamish Henderson, is such a one, telling of the gift of miraculous skill in piping bestowed on an untalented and despised member of that famous family. In Campbell's story of the *Smith's Son Rescued from the Fairies* the boy is given skill with iron work, even though the fairies are frightened of cold iron. Evans Wentz collected a tale from a Barra piper of a fairy gift of skill in carpentry, which again shows the fairy habit of haunting dwellings and workshops. (1967, p. 120)

The skill of musicianship is bestowed as opposed to taught. Acquisition occurs in a flash, on an all or nothing basis: an untalented individual suddenly acquires "miraculous skill," as quick as lightning. This sudden acquisition may occur in adulthood or early childhood. Age seems irrelevant, yet Spence notes that fairies may also "preside over birth and can confer talents on children" (1948, p. 146).

Spence also points out how fairies themselves do not acquire magical power, but instead their magic is instilled naturally:

> The fairy race is inalienably associated with magic and illusion. ... No difference seems to exist between that species of magic practiced by the fairies and that employed by mortals; but magical power would seem to be the natural heritage of the fairy race, who do not have to acquire it as mortals do. (1948, p. 152)

As described above, once practiced, the magic of fairies and mortals may be aligned, but the manner of its acquisition remain worlds apart.

Spence reflects on characteristics of fairy magic that are associated with illusion:

> The fairies were believed to initiate certain favoured folk into knowledge of the magical arts. ... The most characteristic among the arts of fairy magic, perhaps, is that of illusion, enchantment, or, to employ its expressive Scottish synonym, 'glamourie.' This, as the term imparts, was a delusion of the senses of the beholder, the casting of a species of mirage over places and objects to make them seem other than they actually were. A hut or a shieling might, under the power of illusion, appear as a castle or palace, a puddle of water as its moat, rags as resplendent attire and leaves or beans as golden coin. In the event, the gorgeous scene usually vanished

with extraordinary suddenness, leaving the disillusioned beholder in a moss or a ditch. The sudden casting of a mist over the landscape by a fairy when pursued is a notion having the same origin. (1948, p. 153)

This art of illusion often involves "riches composed of whithered leaves and heath-flowers, tufts of hair, pebbles and thin slates," but eventually the spell wears off, revealing rubbish (Spence, 1948, p. 220). Spence also reflects on tales of fairy money "fabricated by magic art" that appear quite real during transactions but later turn into fungus (1948, p. 219). Eventually, illusion erodes, as glamourie does not withstand time, it borrows time.

Perhaps it is unsurprising that the land of fairy takes us farther afield from familiar or commonplace metaphors for learning. The land of fairy, itself a realm of illusion that is never quite apprehensible by its wanderers or observers, establishes a framework for learning which relates concepts quite removed from those we typically grapple with. To be in conversation with the fairies is perhaps unique because it does not place its subjectivity squarely on a learner, but rather distributes it evenly in the environment as a perceived ulterior and often impenetrable space. To this end, the fairies themselves become the recipients of any rewards resulting from bestowed gifts or magic: "J. G. Campbell remarks that a peculiarity of fairy gifts is that 'the benefit of the gift goes ultimately to the fairies themselves, or ... the fruit of it goes into their own bodies'" (Spence, 1948, p. 211).

To communicate with or even observe this land, participants or seekers must pay dues that are not always in primary service of the learner, but in fact benefit the realm itself, letting one become subject to a reality quite apart from that which they will typically tread. Fairyland perhaps offers a transactional form of teaching and learning, requesting curiosity in return for inspiration.

Fairyland amplifies the proverbial idea of wandering, while prioritizing an acute and reverent attention to nature and the myriad wonders of nature. Perhaps fairyland teaches us to romanticize hinterland, to curiously embark on quests beyond known boundaries, to respect nature and give reverence to (and never under-estimate) the powers of nature and otherness. Fairies require a radical stance in terms of acknowledging the relationship of knowledge to the concept of empathy, imbuing nature with inhabitants that honor the power of the natural world – seen and unseen – comprehensive, cryptic, and puzzling. In fairyland, engagements with nature and magic require wonder, curiosity, and a relinquishing of the banal and the mundane. Perhaps fairyland serves as a metaphor for pedagogies which mitigate the space between ourselves and our conception of and experience of time and nature. The land of Fae is a space that is quintessentially other, apart not just from the seeker of its borders, but in fact from the entire assumed structure of one's reality, and this makes any interaction with it fraught with illusion and peril that must be carefully navigated.

We are taught by the fairies, as depicted in folklore and fiction, that to successfully communicate or learn their ways, one must display willingness to spiral into a deep attention of the natural world and grant homage to the non-human world. Fairyland and the fairy archetype codifies the need for generosity of attention in order to gain knowledge and magical favors, as well as a relinquishment of empiric values and logic – this presents models for learning outside of the familiarity or comfort of inherent structures. Fairyland is portrayed as a fleeting experience, full of heightened pleasures and possible perils, existing as transformative alterity. Inherent in the transactional nature of this relationship with the fairies is a realization of one's supplicant status to his or her environment, which can momentarily shift from beneficent to hazardous. This is a status which remains as true today as it may have been in the times form which the fairy lore is sourced, and seeking the whimsical modes of learning that the fairies ask of us is not fruitless. Fairy magic can be reciprocal, and balance must always be maintained in order to bring forth the goal of gaining favor from these beings; in return, one may be bestowed with magic, luck, skills, and knowledge. Accessing the realm of fairies is not simply about being transported for escape and self-enchantment, but forefronts the importance of desire and wandering, while acknowledging the delicacy of give-and-take. Traversing the boundaries of fairyland elevates the values of generosity, wonder, creativity, and curiosity to encounter the multitudes of the natural world and travel beyond the fields we know.

Acknowledgement

This chapter is a revised version of Razdow, K. A. (2004). *Enchanted pedagogy: Archetypal forms, magic, and the transmission of knowledge in fantasy literature* [Unpublished Ed.D. dissertation]. Teachers College, Columbia University.

References

Briggs, K. (1967). *Fairies in tradition and literature*. Routledge & Kegan Paul Limited.
Calvino, I. (2004). Definitions of fantasy: Territory. In D. Sander (Ed.), *Fantastic literature: A critical reader* (pp. 133–134). Praeger Publishers.
Chesterton, G. K. (2004). Fairy tales. In D. Sander (Ed.), *Fantastic literature: A critical reader* (pp. 70–74). Praeger Publishers.

Dunsany, L. (1999). *The King of Elfland's daughter*. The Random House Publishing Group.

Jackson, R. (1981). *Fantasy: The literature of subversion*. Routledge.

Le Guin, U. K. 2004. From Elfland to Poughkeepsie. In D. Sander (Ed.), *Fantastic literature: A critical reader* (pp. 144–155). Praeger Publishers.

MacDonald, G. (1970). *Phantastes*. Ballantine Books.

Olsen, L. (1987). *Ellipse of uncertainty: An introduction to postmodern fantasy*. Greenwood Press.

Rothfuss, P. (2011). *The wise man's fear*. Daw Books, Inc.

Spence, L. (1948). *Fairy tradition in Britain*. Rider and Company.

Tolkien, J. R. R. (1953). *Tree and leaf*. HarperCollins.

CHAPTER 19

Medusa

Alicia Smith

> Medusa once had charms; to gain her love
> A rival crowd of envious lovers strove.
> They, who have seen her, own, they ne'er did trace
> More moving features in a sweeter face.
> Yet above all, her length of hair, they own,
> In golden ringlets wav'd, and graceful shone.
> Her Neptune saw, and with such beauties fir'd,
> Resolv'd to compass, what his soul desir'd.
> In chaste Minerva's fane, he, lustful, stay'd,
> And seiz'd, and rifled the young, blushing maid.
> The bashful Goddess turn'd her eyes away,
> Nor durst such bold impurity survey;
> But on the ravish'd virgin vengeance takes,
> Her shining hair is chang'd to hissing snakes.
> (Ovid's Metamorphoses, Book IV)

In Indigenous understanding, the purpose of stories is to repeat them. And in so doing, participate in the cycle of renewal of them and their sacred knowledge. As a person who carries the history of the Aztec People, and the Greco-Roman people, I have always felt a deep affinity for Snake-Women. Medusa's story is married in my mind as one of protection and cyclical knowledge.

When we first meet her she is a beautiful woman, finding meaning through service to the divine. But not just any divinity, a feminine one, Athena, the Goddess of Wisdom, Warfare and Justice. It is while fulfilling her ceremonial duties, in some accounts sweeping the steps of the temple just like Coatlicue, that Medusa was sexually assaulted.

From Ovid we learn that the first person to ever touch her body, did so without her consent. And it wasn't just anyone, it was a God. According to Bassel van der Kolk, there are two components to a traumatic experience: the terror itself, and not feeling like one can escape it. What can a mortal do to defend themselves against an all-powerful being? What is a priestess to a God? When

© ALICIA SMITH, 2024 | DOI:10.1163/9789004681507_019

one realizes that no matter how hard they fight, that their circumstances will not change, they experience the deepest helplessness and despair.

It is said by some that in a last act of desperation, she cried out to her goddess for salvation, and in return was given what was regarded by the men who transcribed the tale, as a "curse." They insist that Athena ascribed to patriarchal standards of justice and blamed the female victim. In their ignorance, they believed that this wise and powerful being was also so prudish or perhaps more insidiously, jealous, she took this assault as a moral failing on her priestess. The assassination on Medusa's character unfortunately did not end there. Throughout time, again and again she has been retraumatized. Sigmund Freud called Medusa's head a castrated man, or the terror induced by boy's first sight of a woman's vulva. Again and again, using her image to emphasize the supremacy of men and the social order of the genders.

In indigenous culture, we understand that some stories are not meant for the ears of men, let alone their interpretation, and that is why every woman on Earth knows this version is deeply flawed. We know in our bones this was not a curse. In her screaming face we can almost hear her final prayer for deliverance. We know that Athena of all people would have understood it loud.

Western Patriarchy demands all women must adhere to a certain set of prescribed beliefs and behaviors. It insists that a woman's only purpose in life is to be beautiful, accommodating, and attentive to the needs of others. When women are noncompliant with these standards they are ostracized, villainized and made monstrous. The worst kind of woman, the culture says, is aware and independent of this.

All survivors will tell you that their traumas fundamentally changed them. These changes are seldom static and shift and integrate within us through time. We become hypersensitive, and our reactions easily excitable. Triggered. Whether those reactions are to fight, to flee, or to fawn. In her story, Medusa doesn't just shed her skin physically but supernaturally. And in that transformation she embodies something profound. The rage that rises up in survivors that demands recompense for the damage done to them. This rage is the first voice that rails against the victim's guilt and denial. This righteous rage is extremely sacred.

Her existence becomes one of unwavering boundaries. Though many will call those boundaries outsized. Gaslit by a culture that always emphasizes the reaction over what caused it. Perhaps it was drastic. Her golden hair turned to hissing serpents. A woman covered in misembodied phalices. A woman in drag. No one is able to look upon her face without turning to stone. In media she is often depicted as bare breasted, mammalian, enticing to the lecherous gaze of men. But from her hips, emerges a long snake tail. Cold-blooded, reptilian, unrapable. An apotropaic being. Like many women, she found refuge in becoming more terrifying than what caused her terror.

Further, Medusa wasn't just any mortal woman. She was the daughter of Phorcys and Ceto. Cthonic, subterranean, primordial gods, the first born of Gaia. In this sense she was high-born, or more accurately low-born. Athena could have transfigured her into anything, but she chose an asp to hybridize her form. Snakes, who lives their lives with their heart on the Earth, one of the closest beings in all of creation to the Great Mother. Snake, who molts just as those with a uterus, have the ability to transmute all poisons into medicine. As a matter of fact, the snakes that wrap around the medical staff, the Rod of Asclepius, are actually from Medusa's head.

This denotes what I see as a kind of transcultural understanding of the realm of the feminine as keepers of kinship with the nonhuman. This is what Jungian psychoanalysts refer to as the "Wild Woman" archetype. This is healing through a reconciliation with her birthright and her inherent nature. Through her transformation and integration, she finds wholeness, restoration and vitality again. The completion of the cycle.

Great Mother alone has the power to transmute all suffering, it is through reconnection to her, we all find our deepest healing. Snake-Women carry this knowledge from one culture to the next. And it is this knowledge of these cycles that must be protected as well as they protect us. Let us be sure we renew the right stories.

CHAPTER 20

The Golem

On Language and Becoming

Janaka Stucky

The Golem myth is the myth of Creation; it is the injection of soul (*ruah*) into inert matter wherein we are both conduit and creator. This concept of introducing life where life previously did not exist has sparked centuries of Western imagination – from the Alchemical homunculus, to Frankenstein's monster, to Google's potentially sentient AI (De Cosmo, 2022). At the same time, with its recurring motif of flesh and clay, the Golem silently orbits around the assertion that there is a pervasive tellurian earth-spirit which is occluded from us but always already available to fill our mundane vessels (Scholem, 1965b, p. 18).

Just as Adam was an unfinished 'golem' until God breathed life into him, the things we create are inanimate objects until imbued with spirit – a spirit not created by us, but rather that exists beyond our cognition and is channeled through our efforts, whether by science or magic or art, into the Thing which exists with *nefesh hayah*, a living soul.

⋯

We create because we feel "the vast and shapeless melancholy of having been created" (Lispector, 2012, p. 18), and we need a vessel to hold the shared agony of being separated from the sacred Nothing. The Golem is our child, our fictional character, everything we wanted to be but never were. Tireless. Inspired. Divine. The waves of the sea. The buzz and hum of the Word, like one hundred thousand black and golden bees, moving the earth in the shape of a man. We breathe into the Golem and the Golem becomes animated, and it surpasses us.

⋯

Weary of the ever-present trembling ellipses of Now, through the comma of the Golem the period of the I is transmuted into the exclamation of the Thou.

⋯

But the artificial or magical construct is always lacking in some essential function – the story in the Talmud of a Golem who could not speak; the monster who cannot regulate its emotions; the AI whose logic impedes its empathy and destroys us all. As conduits of the divine, creators of breath, we are obsessed with the Golem as a cautionary tale about wielding knowledge absent of either morality (in modern tellings) or mystical purity (in scriptural tellings). As the great Jewish scholar Gershom Scholem points out, the idea of the Golem has evolved over centuries. It "… starts out as a legendary figure. Then it is turned into the object of a mystical ritual of initiation … Then in the whisperings of the profane it degenerates once more into a figure of legend" (Scholem, 1965b, p. 174).

Throughout these permutations, at root the Golem is an ontological struggle: if we are exceptional in some way, in possession of magical power, can we thus create beings with our own magic? "The creation of a Golem is then in some way an affirmation of the productive and creative power of Man" (Scholem, 1965a) … and by extension, the death of God.

• • •

Though we die without death symbolizing us, when we create the Golem the Golem becomes the act that represents us.

• • •

The Golem, above all, is empirically good at existing.

• • •

In 1965 Gershom Scholem heard that the Weizmann Institute at Rehovoth in Israel had completed the building of a new computer, and told Dr. Chaim Pekeris – who created the computer – that it should be named Golem, No. 1 ("Golem Aleph"). In Scholem's own words at its dedication ceremony in 1966:

> The Golem has always existed on two quite separate planes. The one was the plane of ecstatic experience where the figure of clay, infused with all those radiations of the human mind which are the combinations of the alphabet, became alive for the fleeting moment of ecstasy, but not beyond it … [and] The Golem, instead of being a spiritual experience of man, became a technical servant of man's needs, controlled by him in an uneasy and precarious equilibrium. (Scholem, 1965a)

Whether in the classic folktale of the Golem of Prague, or in the modern telling of *The Terminator*, in the Golem's disastrous devolution into technical servitude we come to understand that the value of creating the Golem is in the work itself, not in the product. As a form of mystical work, rabbis of legend would enter ecstatic states to attempt the creation of the Golem – less to animate the clay than to transcend the clay of profane existence – and enter into the immanesecent breath of the World. But when the purpose of the work becomes focused on the constructed outcome rather than simply to attain these mystical experiences, we are threatened with destruction by the very thing we create.

• • •

In the ecstatic state of creation, we pass through the veil which shrouds our dreams and enter into the archetypal world, where we experience great visions of utopia – where whales swim on the waves of song and we are relieved from our labor by silent, tireless automatons. In its highest outcomes, forming the Golem and bringing it to life represents the birth of consciousness from this other world; the "prisoning of the Sea" (Fossum, 2017, p. 249) with the divine names we receive in that realm which we recite over the clay in our earthly world.

• • •

Isaac Luria, the 'father' of contemporary Kabbalah, interpreted the act of creating the Golem as a completely divine act in which "the magically created man has the highest spiritual capacity, which is not to be found, automatically, even in a normally created man ... Moreover, the artificially created anthropoid comprises [for R. Isaac] the whole range of creation, and therefore it is parallel to the divine creation of the world" (Idel, 1990, p. 110). This corresponds to the midrashic tradition where the whole universe is included in Adam, and to Lurianic Kabbalah, where "Adam Qadmon, the Primeval Man, includes the whole range of worlds, and is connected ... to the creation of an anthropoid" (Idel, 1990, p. 111).

• • •

Each of us sees only as much of the world as our nature allows us to see. In creating the Golem, a supernatural being, our vision of the world becomes supernatural.

• • •

We create the Golem to assuage our solitude in labor, in pursuit of perfecting the whole, in pursuit of complete rest. And in creating the Golem we are brought within proximity to the Solitude of God.

∴

It was in this spirit that I set out on my own journey to unlock the heavenly gates and intentionally witness the merkavah while not only retaining my life, my body, and my mind,[1] but also transcribing the pith of that experience – preserving in some form its ecstasis – and creating a book which could then transmit even a fragment of that consciousness to others. My book (Stucky, 2019) became my Golem, an ecstatic dialogue with the Divine greater than the I or Thou alone, which always already threatens to destroy me.

Unlike Bezalel – chief architect and artisan of the Tabernacle, who was in charge of building the Ark of the Covenant "and who knew the combinations of letters with which heaven and earth were made" (Scholem, 1965b, p. 174) – I lack a formal education in the cryptonames of God. My only training in the creative power of letters comes from two degrees in poetry and over a decade of writing verse from trance states. But in finding my own lyrical path to creating a Golem, it seemed to me that deconstructing the relationship between signifier and signified within the crucible of the image was nonetheless in-step with the intentionally fragmented and incomplete form of the Torah. For "No one knows its [right] order, for the sections of the Torah are not given in the right arrangement. If they were, everyone who reads in it might create a world, raise the dead, and perform miracles. Therefore the order of the Torah is hidden and is known to God alone."[2]

∴

The Golem lives in the atmosphere of the miraculous. The miracle being the final simplicity of existence. A word made of earth. The electric edge of magic we use to cut free from anguish, hunger, and humiliation.

∴

The Golem moves from language into existence. The Golem would not exist without words.

∴

THE GOLEM

The Golem is the words we forgot.

∙∙∙

If we are to create the Golem responsibly, if we want to survive its genesis, we must know the Golem's body by heart.

∙∙∙

From the position of a poet and a mystic I approach Hebrew scripture as an intentionally dissonant text – the stories as merely gloss wherein the pure logos of the letters are obscured from us, and completely separate from the narrative which has emerged from scrambling them. To place them in a different order would create narrative nonsense, but at the same time unlock their true power. They are elementary letters – pure *stoicheion*,[3] atomic units – which can be assembled into images free from narrative. Images that unlock the psychic vortex of language which, in the words of Ezra Pound, "gives the sense of sudden liberation; that sense of freedom from time limits and space limits" (Pound, 1970, p. 89).

The *Sefer Yetzirah* describes the creation of "twenty-two letter-elements" and how "they all return in a circle to the beginning through two hundred thirty-one gates – the number of the pairs that can be formed from the twenty-two elements – and thus it results that everything created and and everything spoken issue from one name." In his analysis of this text, Scholem states that "The affinity between the linguistic theory set forth in the book and the fundamental magical belief in the power of letters and words is obvious" (Scholem, 1965b, p. 169).

∙∙∙

Perhaps the reason that the 'true' formula for creating a Golem remains a secret to this day is because there is no single path to its creation, no single form the Golem may take. The process with which to create the Golem lies within us, occluded like a cataract of the Self.

In clarifying our vision of ourselves, in seeing fully the dream of our existence, abysmic and prodigious – disarticulated, miraculous and transient – we unlock the brilliant radii of the two hundred thirty-one gates. The profound intimacy of being.

∙∙∙

The Golem is a memory of happiness arising from the abyss, body brimming with diaphanous emeralds, dust of rubies, and a great pearl of longing. A whiff of woodsmoke on the vagrant breeze. A star lit at dusk above the earth's topaz crown. An open parenthesis begging to be closed with which we are in full communion.

...

The Golem is always becoming. It is our great adventure in which we risk ourselves at every instant.

...

We ask with agony, "Am I alone in the miracle of my being?" and the Golem – a companion, a child, a work of art, a process, a dialogue – is given back to us as the terrible answer of the world.

Notes

1 Merkavah and Kabbalsitic literature is rife with warnings about such an undertaking. For example, take this passage from the Hechaloth Rabbati ("The Great Chambers") where Rabbi Ishmael, who ascends to the Merkavah, hears about the exploits of a previous mystic, Rabbi Akiva: "The Holders of the Throne, the Cherubim, the Wheels and the Holy Living Creatures sing these six melodies, each in a voice stranger and more excellent than the one before it. He who hears the first voice is immediately stricken with folly and madness. He who hears the second voice is lost and never returns. He who hears the third voice is stricken with a fit and dies immediately. The skull of he who hears the fourth voice shatters, and his bones become detached from each other. He who hears the fifth voice gushes forth as water spills from an uncovered jug, and he turns into a pool of blood. The heart of he who hears the sixth voice stings, and his stomach turns and he desires nothing but to be pure as water … Rabbi Akiva heard all these melodies when he ascended to the Merkavah, and he learned them and memorized them from when the servants of the Lord were singing before him."
2 Midrash Tehillim to Psalm 3, ed. S. Buber, 17a.
3 For more, see Plato's *Theaetetus*.

References

De Cosmo, L. (2022, July 12). Google engineer claims AI chatbot is sentient: Why that matters. *Scientific American*.

Fossum, J. E. (2017). *The name of god and the angel of the Lord: Samaritan and Jewish concepts of intermediation and the origin of Gnosticism*. Baylor University Press.

Idel, M. (1990). *Golem: Jewish magical and mystical traditions on the artificial anthropoid*. SUNY Press.

Lispector, C. (2012). *A breath of life*. New Directions.

Pound, E. (1970). Vorticism. In *Gaudier-Brzeska: A memoir*. New Directions.

Scholem, G. (1965a, January). *The golem of Prague & the golem of Rehovoth*. Commentary.

Scholem, G. (1965b). The idea of the golem. In *On the Kabbalah and its symbolism*. Schocken Books.

CHAPTER 21

Hekate

Goddess for the Twenty-First Century

Kay Turner

> It matters which stories tell stories, which concepts think concepts. Mathematically, visually, and narratively, it matters which figures, figure figures, which systems systematize systems.
> DONNA HARAWAY (2016, p. 101)

∴

Many years ago as I was giving up the (holy) ghost of my Presbyterian upbringing, I became interested in the goddesses prevalent in various ancient cultures who had been obscured, demoted and then erased by Church triumphalism. This was mainly accomplished by the cruel work of un-telling old stories and replacing them with new ones. An example from one of the early patriarchs suffices to demonstrate their absolute contempt for female deities – Isis, Athena, Selene, and so many others – who they were bent on ridding from the annals of belief. In his *First Apology*, Justin disparages Athena as a false imitator:

> they spoke of Athena as a daughter of Zeus, but not as a result of intercourse – since they knew that God designed the creation of the world by order of the Word, they spoke of Athena as the first Concept. This we consider very ridiculous, to offer the female form as the image of an intellectual concept. (Richardson, 1970, p. 285)

Oh, yes, the ridiculousness of it all…

Along with other second wave feminists such as Merlin Stone, Carol, Christ, Cristina Biaggi, and Charlene Spretnak, my response to the goddess holocaust was devoted reclamation. In 1976 I founded *Lady-Unique-Inclination of the Night*, a journal of art and the goddess, with the goal of restoring attention to images, both old and new, that held the visual histories and stories of the divine feminine. Writing in 1980 about the journal's mission I said,

> The major concern of *Lady-Unique* is to explore and expand the positive meaning and political efficacy of a feminine aesthetic based originally in the image of the goddess. This aesthetic presents the oldest, continuous tradition of feminine imagery as a vital source of cultural and social information and transformation. (1980, p. 4)

I haven't changed my belief in the unending intellectual and intuitive powers of art and imagination. I don't believe in the gods, but I do believe in their make believe: the magic of their instruction conjured in their stories and the stories we tell about them and with them.

Great importance lies in the image and how it affects and stimulates imagination, from the same etymological origin. Art and the goddess entwined long ago and still interlink today. Both are good to think with and to know. Together they charter our understanding of what life is and can be. The ancient goddesses housed on their altars acted as a cognitive stimulus, a template. The poet Judy Grahn suggests that "Goddess icons embody ideas as the primary motive for their existence." They are what she called "metaforms" or "containers of ideas" (1997, p. 541).

More recently, Donna Haraway demanded consideration of a new epoch founded in deeper recognition of what she calls "symchthonic forces and powers": "I insist that we also need a name for the dynamic ongoing symchthonic forces and powers of which people are a part, within which ongoingness is at stake" (2016, p. 101). Haraway catalogues the proper names of these forces: Gaia, Medusa, Oya, Spider Woman, Raven and many more. I add Hekate to this list, avowing the necessity for our time of tracing her force field, her many names, her instructions left to us in the fragments of myths, histories, invocations, hymns, and magical papyri dating from circa 800 BCE–400 CE. If "[i]t matters which stories tell stories, which concepts think concepts" (Haraway, 2016, p. 101), Hekate's is one such story telling stories that birth a range of transformative ideas, images, and feelings. These can activate our consciousness of "ongoingness" and, as important, our desire to preserve it.

I know Hekate primarily through my long-term devotional and performative study of the Demeter and Persephone myth. Told in full in the Homeric Hymn to Demeter (ca. 700 BCE), this great Greek story of seasonal death and regeneration, in which Hekate plays a significant part, was ritually enacted each year at a temple complex at Eleusis near Athens. The myth reveals important details of Hekate's nature. A cave dweller, she stays hidden but alert to need. From her cave, she is the only one to hear Persephone's piercing cries as she is abducted by Hades. She relieves Demeter's sorrowful search for her child by telling her where her daughter is; and she is there to embrace Persephone in the moment of her release and return to her mother. Her double-fisted torches light up the darkness of the Underworld. As the goddess who opens and closes its entrance, she became Persephone's escort in her annual journey to Hades and back. I annually explore this myth with friends in a winter Solstice celebration I have held since the early 1970s. Over the years, I came to see Hekate as central to this profound story of regeneration. Quite simply it is she who rolls the wheel of cyclical separation and return. Concentrating here on some of what we know of Hekate's beginnings before the Christian era, my primary sources, in English translation, are the "Homeric Hymn to Demeter" (ca. 700 BCE), Hesiod's Theogony (ca. 800 BCE) and the Orphic "Invocation to Hekate" (ca. 200 BCE), with helps from contemporary Greek classicists.[1] These texts disclose essential concepts associated with Hekate's particular regenerative office. I focus on her liminal and mediating character revealed in the widely-applied epithets used by Classic-era Greeks to invoke her as "Goddess of the Crossroads," "Key-holder," "Torch-bearer," and ultimately "Goddess of Thresholds."[2] Johnston suggests that mediation and transmission remained Hekate's greatest functions even as the roles and duties that express them evolved over time: "But the concept behind these duties was at heart the same: from early times, Hekate was the deity who could aid men at points of transition, who could help them to cross boundaries," whether these were of a mundane or extraordinary nature, or later a magical one (1990, pp. 73–74). Our deeper understanding of Hekate's performance as goddess of crossroads and thresholds is so greatly needed now.

1 Hekate's Lineage

Hekate's role as a goddess of passage is borne out in her lineage. What I offer here is in no way definitive, but I follow what I consider the most telling version of her genealogy in order to situate Hekate's story in other overlapping stories that reveal her cause. A very old goddess with roots in Mesopotamian, Hittite, Phrygian, and Egyptian moon and earth cults such as that of Ereshkigal, the Babylonian goddess of the underworld, in Theogony, Hesiod sets her up as a bridge between the preceding Titan gods and the new Olympians. She retains realms of earth, sea, and atmosphere that have belonged to her "since the beginning" (lines 423–425). Hekate holds a "unique position as inheritor of three cosmic realms Pontos (Sea), Gaia (Earth), Uranus (Sky), and who sums up in her person all of the preceding cosmogony and theogony" (Clay, 1984, p. 32). The reverence accorded to her by Zeus implicates her strong link to the past – the deep past of creation itself. Considered essential in the sense of emanating from the beginning, she is also outside the patriarchal order of Olympus. Unowned by it, she creates alliances with whom she chooses. Hekate serves no one by demand, not even Zeus.

Hekate's domain is traced along a slanted path of ascent and descent that describes constant movement from the underworld of shades and ghosts, above to her earthly cave and seat at the Crossroads, to her travels among restless souls who exist between the Earth and Moon. With her Keys to the Kozmos, she opens the gates between life-giving realms of earth, water, and air, and unites them all in the flow of her comings and goings: ever fluid, ever in motion through the realms she oversees and protects.

Hekate's Greek family history starts with great-grandmother Gaea, the primeval earth goddess who pairs with her great-grandfather, Uranus, god of the sky to produce Hekate's grandmother Phoebe. A moon goddess associated with prophecy, who could fly, and was said to "conjure a silver light," Phoebe's magnetism lends her the ability to attract and repel objects.[3] Phoebe pairs with Hekate's grandfather Coeus, a Titan of great intellect and inquisitive mind, and they produce two daughters, Leto and Asteria. Leto, births Hekate's cousins, Artemis and Apollo. Beautiful Asteria, associated with falling stars and oneiromancy (dream prophecy and interpretation) unites with Perses, the Titan god called the Ravager, who is associated with the constellations Aries and Sirius, the Dogstar. Hesiod also refers to Perses as "preeminent among all men in wisdom." This starry pair have but one child: Hekate.

An only child usually would be stigmatized, but for Hekate this status instead defines her singularity, recognized even by Zeus. Hesiod states: "... because she is an only child, the goddess receives not less honor, but much more still, for Zeus honors her" (Hesioid, 1914, line 428). And again: "So, then, albeit her mother's only child, she is honored amongst all the deathless gods" (line 450). Greatly revered and largely autonomous, Hekate is the deification of a woman who has owned a room of her own since time began. This is important. She carries the title *mounogenēs* (Gr) meaning only begotten, but also, as Clay suggests, carrying the sense of unique being, one and only (1984, p. 32). Along these lines, Froma Zeitlin maintains that Hekate remains "ever virgin" and that she creates "no new genealogical line" (1996, p. 75). Several of her titles indicate her matchless primacy: "Unconquerable," "Untamable," "Indomitable," and "Eternal."

Though regularly associated with the chthonic, or underworld realm, her lineage underscores the complexity of Hekate's wide-ranging stewardship. Her Titan family collectively includes elemental earth and sky, moon, and stars. That her great-grandmother Gaea and great-grandfather Uranus constitute earth and sky as the basis of our planetary reality gives Hekate a charge, from the very beginning, to serve as a guardian of creation. Significantly her parentage is night-sky derived: great-grandfather, grandmother, mother, father. She feels at home in darkness but she also brings light. Her relationship to the oracular underworld comes through her moon goddess grandmother, Phoebe, whose lunar associations also include the casting of silvery light. Her mother and father lend the brightness of starlit nights.

Hekate's well-known epithet, "Torch Bearer," may stem from lunar associations, including her occasional identity as a moon goddess. Many of the Greek gods and goddesses are depicted with torches. A common source of night light when moving from place to place, the vernacular torch achieves new meaning when transferred to symbolic status. Unlike any other deity, Hekate carries two torches. She brings a brighter, penetrating light to Demeter's search for Persephone. The despairing mother "encountered Hecate carrying brightness, Held in her hands" (Weigle, 2007, p. 103). That Hekate joins Demeter on the 10th day of her quest suggests a lunar connection to her torches. Hekate in her aspect as waning moon remains hidden in darkness for a third of the month; as waxing moon, her luminous phase sources the fire light of her torches. That a goddess of darkness, ghosts, and death also provides augmented light to Demeter demonstrates Hekate's contradictory nature, her determined absorption and unification of binary opposites, darkness and light, death and life.

Her nocturnal sky lineage also grants Hekate a position of ineffable distance observed in her trait of gracious detachment. A popular origin of her name comes from the Greek word hekatos meaning "worker from afar" (d'Este & Rankine, 2009, p. 13). Yet she compliments distance with the closeness of her work on behalf of all who seek her mediation.

Key gifts given to Hekate out of her line include intellect, wisdom, intuition, prophecy, the ability to fly, and the power to destroy. Hekate comes into the Olympian world with many hereditary talents and the will to exercise them. Her knowledge of old family stories trains her intelligence, intuition and compassion. For example, both her mother's and aunt's narratives highlight their escapes from seduction and rape. After the fall of the Titans, beautiful Asteria was pursued all over the world by Zeus. Though she scorned him, he relentlessly persisted. She eludes him finally by transforming herself into a quail, which dives into the sea only to be chased by lascivious Poseidon. So, she then transforms herself into the island Delos, where her sister Leto takes shelter from jealous Hera to give birth to Artemis and Apollo (Theoi Project, 2023). Hekate, already born, retains foreknowledge of unwanted male pursuit and its potential result in abduction and rape. From mother's to daughter's story a transfer is made of wariness and anxiety concerning the intentions of male gods. Hekate comes fully prepared to play her salvific role in the Demeter and

Persephone myth. She hears Persephone's cries of alarm as an echo of her mother's.

Perhaps if properly understood, the myth of Demeter and Persephone should be called that of Demeter, Persephone *and* Hekate.[4] Cast in the light of this trivium, Hekate, who activates crucial aspects of the plot, significantly allies with Demeter in her recovery of Persephone. Together they reverse the incestuous greed of Zeus and his brother Hades, restoring the mother/daughter bond as it both represents and perpetuates natural reproduction and fertile earth in the rhythmic cycle of growth and withering, give and take. Hekate, widely propitiated in her office as "Caretaker of the Young" and "Protector of Children," proves a perfect ally in Persephone's rescue. But she herself is not a mother. Zeitlin maintains that her role as caretaker shifts the female concept of fecundity from birthing to nurturance, from reproduction to care that is not necessarily maternal but universally required (1996, p. 77). Hekate also exhibits her own powers of sustainable increase and decrease of food sources, livestock and fish among them. She parallels Demeter whose dominion largely comprises florae and grain. Separately and together, Hekate and Demeter condemn rapaciousness and depredation, both sexual and agricultural. Their partnership and its effects are critical for interpreting the connection between the rape of women and rape of the land and sea, in other words between #MeToo and #ClimateCrisis.

Hekate's other analogs, correspondents, and opposites include Artemis, who plays a more prominent part in Greek religion as it evolves, but who is often aligned or doubled with her cousin. They live in the same family house. Hekate, mirrors Artemis, another virginal goddess, and is always within Artemis. She shares traits with the liminal messenger god Hermes, too. Both are boundless. As important, the record shows little association between Hekate and the other Olympian goddesses Hera, Athena, Hestia, and Aphrodite. These conceptualize marriage, domesticity, politics, and sex. Hekate's ways are different; her agenda contrasts with theirs. Her layered difference, overall her queerness in the old meaning of that term as slanted or athwart, gives Hekate access to the advantages of marginality, liminality, ambivalence, and mystery as implicated in certain of her titles.

2   Goddess of the Crossroads

The "Orphic Hymn to Hekate" (ca. 200 BCE) opens with, "I call Hekate of the Crossroads, worshipped at the meeting of three paths, oh lovely one." One of her most widely invoked titles provides insight into Hekate's advocacy of liminal places, of encounter, of movement, and journey. Traditionally paid homage at earthly crossroads, she insured "safe transition through an uncertain point; she was the factor that bridged the gap imagined to exist there" (Johnston, 1990, p. 74). Liminal energies emanate from crossroads; the meeting point dispenses a charge of the betwixt and between. Nowhere and somewhere at the same time – filled with both fear and options. Which way to go?

A meeting place of uncertainty but also of choice, no wonder offerings were left and petitions made to her at crossroads. Hekate Suppers were sent on the new moon of new beginnings to her statues and shrines found at intersections (Johnston, 1991, p. 219). Feasting her brought protection from the phantoms who dwelled in liminal shadows. But these supplicating meals also invited her guidance for any transition. Certain polluted materials such as corpses were also assigned to crossroads in an attempt to defuse their association with death. But perhaps the food refuse left behind at Hekate's shrines insured that she would use the abject powers of decay to fertilize the cycle of renewal at this site of transition. For Hekate was very much a goddess seated at the crossroads between life and death; present at birth as protector of children and present with the deceased in her titular role as Brimo, who guided the dead from this world into the underworld (d'Este & Rankine, 2009, p. 59). The sorceress Medea invokes Hekate specifically as a goddess capable of the ultimate reversal: "Brimo, the wanderer by night, the subterranean goddess of the underworld. She then gave birth in fire: the goddess of death gave birth" (Zeitlin, 1996, pp. 92–93).

If we generally conceive of a crossroads as the convergence of two roads, or the centrum of the axis, Hekate's crossroads offers an addition. For as Goddess of the Trivium, she is at the meeting of three roads. Hekate's powers activate that liminal point of conjunction, liberating the four quarters by an act of the power of three. Obviously the actual crossing of three roads is not so unusual, but the concept, as it names this goddess, is indeed special. Three destabilizes the certainty of one and two, of mono and dyad. Three rejects stasis in favor of vitality. The power of three is utilized in ritual and magic to activate. One, two, three and done. Because she is a bridge from past to present, from old gods to new, she is always leading the way on a third path, the third path of possibility.

A consort of all liminal goddesses and gods, witches, ghosts, and other transitional figures, Hekate opens a deviant path of release from the conventional structural axis. I think of her on her own third path, a crooked one at that, trailing up to the moon and down to the underworld on a slant: goddess of slant, crooked, deviant paths. Fluid in movement between realms, between one place and another, between the living and the dead, between then and now. Friend of ghosts and all things that appear and disappear, a teacher of crossings, going through the gates from one world to another.

Early in the formation of an increasingly more refined human consciousness, Hekate conceptualizes what we might now call a queer worldmaking sensibility: the power of three, the third path utilized to escape binding binary structures into the relief of messiness and fortune out of which newness is made. Hekate of the Trivium invites departure from structural impositions – and the social assumptions they literally engender. Those strict, patriarchally normative divisions that putatively bring chaos to its knees in favor of order, creating the political, religious, and social structures of misogynist power and authority. Our anti-structural, non-binary aspirations are embedded in Hekate's early proposal of a third road journey into Being and the freedom to be.

Hekate may be important to Zeus as a mediator between gods and humans, but she owes no one. The crossroads goddess offers choice because she herself willfully chooses. This Orphic attribute of Hekate, adumbrated centuries earlier in Hesiod saying she does what she wants (lines 440–443), brings into focus her long history of arbitrarily dispensing of her powers to benefit or harm, to give or take away. While all the Olympian gods acted capriciously, she exerts a kind of willfulness and a sense of righteousness that gives pause, even to them. As Hesiod describes, "if she will, she increases from a few, or makes many to be less" (Hesioid, 1914). Yet she receives countless petitions for benefit to humankind. Certainly Hekate is "the one by whose will prayers are fulfilled" (Clay, 1984, p. 35). Unpredictable in her dispensation, yes, but also believed to be beneficent and loyal to regenerative causes – to the need for Persephone's spring, to the abundance of the fisherman's catch, to the lunar cycle of new moon to full. Her willfulness is at the service of protecting and encouraging the life force in all creation. One of her titles affirms this: Nourisher of Life (Gr. *zootropos*). It's a balancing act that may at times seem capricious to humankind but from Hekate's point of view is radically purposive.

For Hekate, though distant, also comes to us intimately as a guide, a bridge, an intermediary. Johnston says her cave-dwelling nature (*Homeric Hymn to Demeter*, line 25) points to this: she lives neither above nor below the earth. Rather, Persephone's caretaker makes her home,

> intermediarily between the two. The guide acts to bridge – either literally or figuratively – two distinct realms in order that the individual may pass from one to the other. So, too, that which is intermediary acts to close the gap between two discreet entities and provide continuity. (Johnston, 1990, pp. 27–28)

3   Goddess of the Threshold

More widely, this goddess of crossroads is a goddess of all thresholds, places of the in-between, sites of transition. At gates and doorways, entry and exit points, any place that shuddered with liminal indeterminacy, shrines were erected in appeal to Hekate's protection and guidance. All over the ancient Greek and Roman landscape and as late as the Byzantine era, archaeological and textual evidence notes the remains of hekataea, pillar shrines placed in front of domestic doorways and city entries. Tellingly, Karl Kerényi says that her great temple at Eleusis, the Hekataion, was situated at the entry point to this site where the Mysteries of Demeter were celebrated (1967, p. 70). All the initiates – thousands of them – passed first through Hekate's sanctuary, asking her blessing, before they proceeded into that most liminally sacred underground space to receive Demeter's gift of renewal. But such renewal begins with Hekate's guardianship and points once again to her partnership with Demeter in bringing the life-death cycle full circle.

For Hekate is the guardian of all thresholds enabling the cycle of separation and return. Demeter and Persephone more commonly represent this cycle but Hekate activates it through what I call her "thresholding" genius. Changing noun to gerund gives us a better sense of Hekate's energetic principle: not only a guardian of thresholds, she is the threshold itself, the galvanizing source of movement and change that insures the life force.

4   Key-Holder

Key-holder or Key-Keeper traditionally describes Hekate as the one who unlocks the doorway to the Underworld, giving dead souls entry to the house of Hades. Also known later in the Orphic tradition as the "Queen who holds the Keys to all the Kozmos" (line 6), Hekate, striding or flying through air, sea, land, stratosphere, and on to the moon, opens the gates that bound these territories, connecting them, and us to them as she goes. The key acts as a metaphor of assurance that opening is possible, that entry will be given. Of course she can lock the gates, too. As Johnston suggests, Hekate's expanded role as key-holder also implicates her in the closing of liminal cosmic boundaries where chaos potentially exerts a destructive de-stabilizing force. By also creating boundaries, she is associated with organizing "chaotic matter by means of establishing limits" (Johnston, 1990, pp. 47–48). She uses her keys judiciously to regulate equilibrium across all the regions over which she presides.

5   Hekate of the 21st Century

How does Hekate's story – her story within stories – matter? If stories tell stories that link to concepts and systems, I have suggested several important ways in which Hekate speaks to twenty-first century urgencies. As the German philosopher Walter Benjamin cried out on behalf of history at the onset of World War II, we must "seize hold of the past as it flashes up at a moment of danger." We must seize hold of Hekate.

A guardian moving effortlessly through her domains even as she dwells simultaneously in all of them, Hekate maps a unified ecosystem of which we are only a small and ultimately disposable part. At this point, her realms are under the relentless threat of human incursion, opportunism, and brutality: razing the rain forests, mining the ocean floor, poisoning the air, eroding the ozone layer, and sending rich white men on rocket ship joy rides to the moon. That greed and avarice upsets natural balance and harmony may strike as a dusty moral cliché, but Hekate reminds us that long before and long after we fail to learn its obligatory lesson, her Kosmic story of death and renewal will prevail, even if we do not. In Nagy's translation of the Homeric Hymn to Demeter, he describes Hekate as "the one who keeps in mind the vigor of nature" (2018, line 24). Her intellect aligns with her concern for primal vitality. A goddess of all matter, and all that matters, Hekate's reign over materiality – the very stuff that comprises all nature and the cosmos – will not end. What is made she unmakes, reverses, and rearranges. Her mandate is change or be changed.

As goddess of thresholds and liminality she encompasses the energies of transition we require. Foretold in the rape and abduction of Persephone, the agonizing search for her and withholding of fruitfulness by her mother Demeter, Hekate enters that story as both a witness and a savior. A quickener of realization and manifestation, her thresholding nature activates all her qualities – intellect and intuition, prophecy and protection, oracular and oneiric – to stimulate the growth of consciousness, to assure ongoingness. Persephone's rescuer left her hidden place to bring the light. Will she do the same for us? We are already seated at the crossroads of a great divide. Even as the axis crumbles, will we choose Hekate's third path of transformation and renewal? Or not?

6   Coda: Hope's Cave

Last summer, walking along a tributary of the Shepaug River in northwest Connecticut, I came to a large granite and gneiss outcropping, oblong in shape.

Jutting out to the trail it created a perfectly inverted V-shaped cave, a gift of the last Ice Age. Shallow, with just room enough to shelter a single person, I sat down inside Hekate's cave. I felt the outline of her presence in the form the rock took thousands of years ago. Not a mystical feeling so much as a simple feeling of recognition of her extension in time, from the past to the present and future. From such a hollow, Hekate heard Persephone's screams. I only hope that she hears ours.

Notes

1 Special thanks to artist Elizabeth Insogna (see her essay in this volume) for many exciting and insightful conversations about Hekate over the past few years.
2 The significant literature on Hekate found in the Chaldean Oracles of the early common era elevates her as "Soul of the Cosmos" (see Johnston, 1990). Eventually she became negatively attributed as "Goddess of Witches." It is still one of her most popular titles today, but with a much more positive slant as demonstrated in numerous recent books and an array of websites (e.g.<keepingherkeys>). Burgeoning interest in Hekate remediates her longtime absence from consideration by scholars, popular writers on Greek religion, and even feminists. There are exceptions – Clay, 1984, Grahn, 1997, Johnston, 1990, Marquardt, 1981, and Zeitlin, 1996 among them – but many pre-1980s texts I have reviewed fail to consider or even mention her in the line-up of primary Greek deities. I venture that in the early modern era, her growing association with spurious or malevolent magic, along with the generally pernicious effects of misogyny, eventually led to erasure.
3 https://mythology.net/greek/titans/phoebe/
4 The strong bond between Demeter, Persephone, and Hekate finds emphasis in the Orphic belief that Hekate was born of Demeter.

References

Clay, J. S. (1984). The Hecate of the theogony. *Greek, Roman, and Byzantine Studies, 25*, 27–38.

d'Este, S., & Rankine, D. (2009). *Hekate: Liminal rites*. Avalonia Books.

Grahn, J. (1997). Marija Gimbutas and metaformic theory: Women as creators of cognitive ideas. In J. Marler (Ed.), *From the realm of the ancestors: An anthology in honor of Marija Gimbutas* (pp. 539–547). Knowledge, Ideas & Trends, Inc.

Haraway, D. (2016). *Staying with the troubles: Making kin in the Chthulucene*. Duke University Press.

Hesiod. (1914). The Homeric hymns and Homerica (H. G. Evelyn-White, Trans.) In *Theogony*. Harvard University Press/William Heinemann Ltd.

Johnston, S. I. (1990). *Hekate Soteira: A study of Hekate's roles in the Chaldean Oracles and related literature*. Scholars Press.

Johnston, S. I. (1991). Crossroads. *Zeitschrift for für Papyrologie und Epigraphik, 88,* 217–224.

Kerényi, K. (1967). *Eleusis: Archetypal image of mother and daughter* (R. Manheim, Trans.). Princeton University Press.

Marquardt, P. A. (1981). A portrait of Hecate. *American Journal of Philology, 102/3,* 243–260.

Nagy, G. (Trans.). (2018). *Homeric hymn to Demeter.* Harvard Center for Hellenic Studies.

Richardson, C. C. (1970). *Early Christian fathers.* Westminster Press.

Theoi Project. (2023). *Asteria's flight from Zeus.* https://www.theoi.com/Titan/TitanisAsteria.html#Cult

Turner, K. (1980). Why we are so inclined. In *Lady-Unique-Inclination-of-the-Night: Journal of Art and the Goddess,* Cycle 5. Sowing Circle Press

Weigle, M. (2007). *Spiders and spinsters* (2nd ed.). Sunstone Press.

Zeitlin, F. (1996). *Playing the other: Gender and society in classical Greek literature.* Chicago University Press.

CHAPTER 22

Fool Party

Meg Whiteford

As Ozzy Osborne wailed, "All aboard! Hahaahahaha!" (Osborne, 1980). Fair winds and following seas! Beware of life in the doldrums, eternal anchor in port! The crew is made up of naysayers, jugglers, stargazers, chatterers, and shapeshifters. They steer their ship, none of them trained, all of them relying on intuitive knowledge, deep into tempestuous waters, unafraid, for fools know what riches lie on the other side of the dividing line: an enlightened journey, the picture seen from outside of repressive structures, and laughter amid all the prismatic, mad angles of life.

And what vessel is this before me in port, you ask? Why, it's the Ship of Fools, a Platonic trope turned into a satirical poem in verse written by Sebastian Brant, a portion of a triptych by Hieronymous Bosch, a novel by Katherine Anne Porter, and a hit Stanley Kramer movie starring Vivien Leigh. All versions lampoon the problems of governance, governmental institutions, and the nature of justice, and each employs satire to consider the flaws of living under that nefarious adage wielded to justify abuses of power: 'it's just the way things are.' But are they? Must things be just the way things are?

In the boat of the Bosch, members of the clergy merrily sing, drink, and pass out (three sheets to the wind) aboard a much too small ship. They're perhaps engaged in a Fête de Fous, a day or week when the clergy switch societal roles and costuming with the fools (the serfs and peasants) of the town to act mad for a day, while the mad act the church, and all are liberated from established caste divisions (Bakhtin, 1984). Think: Quasimodo gracing the streets of Paris from his hideaway in the bell tower, the drama released in all its glory, the start to the story (pardon the rhyme). Below the boat in the deep water swim two naked people, perhaps representing the poor, who beg for sustenance never gifted. And yet, if this is indeed the Fête de Fous, these are more likely depictions of a drowning clergy, i.e. a representation of a desired demise of organized, stodgy Establishment. Down with the ship!

Look closer! Sent up the pole in the halyard ropes dangles a jester (could this be the virago Mad Meg? No relation to the author, or is there?) in breeches and the traditional medieval fool's cap replete with dead donkey ears. The fool sips from a wine goblet. Her requisite specter hangs over her shoulder. Only her scepter's bauble bears a screaming head in an on-the-nose (-neck?) skewering of the Church. From the mainsail grows a tree, most likely the Tree of Knowledge. For those aboard the Ship of Fools, madness represents deep spiritual knowledge rooted to the tree of good and evil as its guiding pole. Without sails, the crew sails forth with only their inner compass, their instincts, to guide them. Whether they'll sink or swim remains unknown. But fate is besides the point of journeys! And guess what else, the word fool comes from the Latin for "bag of wind," i.e. that element which moves the sails upon the water, as in the wind which blew Odysseus's Homeric Galley toward his exploits, and so I'm sure you see where I'm going with this etymological reference!

And of that Tree of Knowledge: how Foolish Eve must have been to pluck the pomegranate from its forbidden branches, as decreed by the voice in her head. Her idiocy released human consciousness. How absolutely bonkers Persephone must have been to eat the pomegranate seeds from Hades, unleashing upon the world the seasons! As evidenced by these halfwits, we see the fools are the scrappiest of archetypes – they take what is available and alchemize the disparate pieces (including themselves) into alternative truths and worlds, thus playing a fundamental role in the magic of transforming as a human. There are cross-cultural examples of further Divine Madness in holy texts of Christianity, Islam, Judaism, Hinduism, and Buddhism. For these divinely mad, their foolishness sanctioned their challenges of social mores as paths toward spirituality, which was often seen as a gift from the gods themselves.

I apologize for referencing Foucault, but I stumbled upon this essay as I was writing my own so I must, for the fool must always improvise off a fluke, but in Michel Foucault's essay "Stultifera Navis," the proverbial and painterial Ship of Fools depicts a journey of the "madmen" exiled on a voyage across the sea and away from the easily spooked and turgid Society of eighteenth-century Britain. Yet Foucault writes,

> Fashion favored the composition of these ships, whose crew of imaginary heroes, ethical models, or social types, embarked on a great symbolic voyage which would bring them, if not fortune, then at least the figure of their destiny or their truth. (Foucault, 1961, pp. 7–8)

Doesn't embarkment always take a bit of foolishness? Who doesn't want a little bit of the figure of truth in their life?

Still, it was and remains hard work to learn to be a fool on a ship of chumps, to bear the brunt of the joke, to sacrifice oneself to temper the power of the nefarious and powerful idiots ruling the vessel upon which we sail. It's dangerous work sticking out in such a homogeneously oriented space such as race, gender, religion, capitalism, or species. Throughout many cultures, the fool's presence signifies irreverence for power and hierarchy, even for the human form – sometimes they appear in the form of a fox as in the Reynard cycle or ravens of the Indigenous peoples of the Pacific Northwest such as the Tlingit. Of course the Shakespearean Fools – think of Puck turning Nick Bottom's top (head) literally into his bottom (as the head of an ass), thus turning the narrative top to bottom and rendering their world topsy turvy, queer.

The fool eases or inflames high stake situations with humor, depending on the day, depending on the decree. Perhaps the best represented of the fools, the jester of the medieval courts soothed social tensions with levity. The cream of the clods would deftly maneuver elite power-hungry temperaments with their sharp, deflating wit. As Foucault says of his madmen (here I interchange the word fool with Foucault's word madman, both characters of folly), "[the fool] stands center stage as the guardian of truth-playing ... if folly leads each man into a blindness where he is lost, the [fool], on the contrary, reminds each man of his truth." It's the fool's job to perform the magic of disorientation, unsettling what we think we know or what we assume we meant to make way for a more pioneering form of knowledge. I'm talking Art here! I like to think of a fool haranguing a mad king as he falls into violent lunacy in an unfortunate, but all too common, role reversal between lunatic and the Man in Charge. Question everything and everyone because every answer is invented by someone, who is not you, and therefore we mad people are just as rightfully kings as anyone else.

If you don't have access to the court, you'll likely find a fool hiding somewhere in all the various institutions in your life. Often they overlap with the mad scientist, or the nutty professor, the drunkard, the troublemaker, or trickster, so look out. There's a lineage, training, to foolishness, an intuitive timing that can be and should be taught through observation and trial and error. Think of the calculus teacher who helped you understand a complicated problem in a nuanced, stimulating way through a joke, or the student who refused to take her chemistry lab tests but instead presented their own musical about the behavior of matter (this was me and yes I was voted class clown. I was also diagnosed with about a half dozen mental illnesses, so I'm intimate with all angles [and angels] of madness/foolishness).

I bestow you with an excerpted ode from Ozzy once more: "I've listened to preachers/I've listened to fools/I've watched all the dropouts/Who make their own rules/One person conditioned to rule and control/The media sells it, and you live the role" (Osborne, 1980). I long ago settled into my role on the Fool's Ship. Not to make it all about me – this is a contemporary essay so why not? – but if you're a funny girl or a funny queer (the fool is inarguably queer, which I think I said before briefly but here I say it again, the fool is queer) or want to be a funny girl, watch Barbara Streisand in *Funny Girl*. This movie was my informal education. This fool is happily, as Barbara as Fanny Brice says, a "bagel on a plate full of onion rolls" (Wyler, 1968). If pedagogy exists within frameworks and institutions such as higher learning and higher education and academia, it seems unlikely a fool could find a seat at the roundtable. They instead offer an autodidactic pedagogy. How, the fool asks whilst standing on her head, can and might we live our lives other than the ways foretold to us, to create differently, to think for ourselves, to become an onion roll? Socrates, who was himself considered a fool, is associated with the vertex *oxyMORON*: "I do not know, do not think that I know either" (Plato, 1901, p. 39). And to admit that one is powerless to ever know anything as absolutely as one knows nothing, well, this is magic wisdom taught only through playing the fool.

And what of the role of magic in all this? Can a fool be said to be magic? Magic can be anything that turns something on its head, a boat on its back, anything which transforms some thing or some idea from one to another, such as: a good joke. If magic serves to create an illusion through a setup and pay off, to hide the bones, a joke reveals the skeleton of, to cudgel the metaphor, the ship. A good joke delights. The strange makes you think. A barmy sets us loose. This is magic worth learning.

References

Bakhtin, M. (1984). *Rabelais and his world*. Indiana University Press.
Foucault, M. (1961). *Folie et déraison: Histoire de la folie à l'âge classique*. Librairie Plon.
Osborne, O. (1980). Crazy train. *Blizzard of Oz, Jet*.
Plato. (1901). *Apology of socrates*. Bloomsbury.
Wyler, W. (Dir.). (1968). *Funny girl*. Columbia Pictures.

CHAPTER 23

Precipitated Spirit Painting and Visionary Space

Erin Yerby

> In an obscure and puzzling way, the artist develops a work of art. As it gains a life of its own, it becomes an entity, an independent spiritual life, which as a being, leads the life of material realism. It is, therefore, not simply a phenomenon created casually and inconsequentially indifferent to spiritual life. Instead as a living being, it possesses creative active forces.
>
> KANDINSKY, *Concerning the Spiritual in Art*

∵

The gallery of Spiritualist portraits covers all four walls in Lily Dale's Assembly Hall. Here, the living and the dead exchange glances. The Spiritualists' emphasis on a dynamic experiential kinship, crossing life and death, is made visible in this frozen archive of faces, mostly photographed, sometimes painted.

During a course in mediumship I was taking, we began with a visualization exercise. Seated in this room of faces, we were to visualize ourselves caught in a thick fog, a fog that would allow us to wait for the spirits' emergence. Sitting very still, eyes closed, hands on lap, feeling the cold of metal collapsible chairs, and surrounded by fifteen other practitioners in the same posture – I took a deep breath. The cloud of fog was gathering. The air felt thick. Opening my eyes, the same fog that had gathered in that inward space – which in our limited way, we sometimes call the mind's eye – was now in three-dimensional space, filling the room. In this moment a woman appeared, as if stepping out of one of the photographs. At once more and less an appearance in the room, her presence was confusing – not only the sensory fact of *a presence*, as one might expect, but that this presence crossed inner and outer vision at one and the same time. She felt real and not quite real, inhabiting a blurry edge of perception.

There is always a looming doubt, even, as it was shared with me, among seasoned mediums, insofar as they must continuously learn to *discern* the work of "my imagination" from spiritual presence. Then again, over the course of my three years of fieldwork training in mediumship, the exercises consistently acknowledged the zone of indiscernibility between imagination and spirit communication. Intentional visualization exercises often begin with an imagined scene, which one is encouraged to unfold and follow – you climb these images like rungs in a ladder, until they intensify, take on a life of their own, and seem to be propelled no longer by 'me' but by some external force. This climb from imagination to spirit, is more akin to crossing thresholds of intensity. In other words, these are the moments when the image – understood as spirit communication – attains a kind of autonomy, and you feel you are no longer in the drivers' seat.

It often struck me that the way the medium carves out an inner space in her body, for the precipitation of images, might be likened to the black box container of a camera: the body gives itself an inner space, in which to intensify (and develop images from) an outer light – and light is what the spirits are often described as. This metaphor is extended in mediumistic practice with the use of the curtained "cabinets," so often used in the 19th century (and to a lesser extent today), wherein the medium would sit in darkness to intensify the forces passing through the body, at times giving 'birth' to strange material compositions, cloud-like shapes known by the scientific sounding term, *ectoplasm*. Of course, analogies to photographic process are deeply embedded within the history of 19th century Spiritualism, not only with the emergence of spirit photography but also in the language, still common today, of mediumistic 'development.'

1   Making Visible What Is Invisible

This mystery of making visible what is invisible, here within a self-consciously 'modern' North American tradition of mediumship, is the subject of this essay. While practices in "mental" mediumship, such as the giving 'messages' to a 'sitter' or offering 'demonstrations' of spirit presence verbally to an audience, are among the more common practices today, the practice of physical mediumship, externalizing spirits or spirit communication in some observable or audible material form (levitations, ectoplasmic expressions, materialized voices, etc.) while much less common, still finds circles of committed practitioners.[1] Or, put another way, physical mediumship might be defined as the mystery by which images that were once within us become externalized entities – *materializations* that seem at once to congeal the affect and energy of the medium, at yet are attributed a material as well as a spiritual autonomy. The implicit echo to artistic practice is an intentional one. One of the greatest examples of physical mediumship found in the history of Spiritualism is in the phenomena known as "precipitated spirit painting," popular during the late 19th and into the early twentieth centuries.

Ron Nagy, a devoted Spiritualist, curator, and personality at large and in charge of the small ramshackle Museum at Lily Dale, wrote a small book on the subject in 2006, defining such spirit painting as the means by which a likeness appears on a canvas "without the use of human hands." Nagy compares precipitated spirit paintings to "other inventions of those times including the telephone, telegraph, Ediphone etc." – inventions "not understood but accepted" (Nagy, 2010, p. 2). The magical sensation around demonstrations of electricity in the 19th century is echoed in Nagy's comparison: mediumship, like electricity, involves what is said to be common to magical actions, as 'action at a distance' – action without direct/visible mediation or contact with what is acted upon. Precipitated painting, mediated by the presence of the medium through whom the spirits act, is said to occur without direct contact of the medium's hands upon the canvas.

Comparing spirit painting to emergent 19th century communication technologies, Nagy reflects a well-worn path within Spiritualism, analogizing what spirit mediums do with emergent communication technologies of modernity.

> The canvas is new and clean. A "pot" of paint is used with all the colors of the spectrum placed in it. No brushes are used or are in the room or area where the séance is taking place. The medium is present, along with the sitter and observers. The séance is usually done by appointment but in many instances, auditoriums were used, and random numbers were drawn to pick the sitter who would be requesting a painting. The spirit entity whom the sitter is mentally requesting to "come through" or appear on the canvas is usually unknown to the medium. The framed canvas is placed on an easel, stood on a table, and lightly held by the medium or mediums, one on each side. In some instances, the canvas is laid flat, facing up on a table with all in attendance placing their palms down on the table around the canvas. The pot of paint is placed in front of or on the floor near the canvas. The lights are dimmed for mood, but never completely darkened. The mediums go into trance and the sitter observers are in a meditative state, completing an energy circle. The sitter mentally visualizes the loved one who has passed on into spirit life and whom they would like to appear. Slowly, like a Polaroid photograph develops, the painting begins to appear. It usually takes fifteen minutes to an hour for the precipitation process to be complete [emphasis added].
> (Nagy, 2010, pp. 2–3)

The painting appears without the agency of eye or hand, interrupting the intimate loop between vision, hand and material belonging to the practice of painting. Here, the image develops like a phantasm, as if by its own agency, unmediated by the artist; the emergence of the figure, likened to the sudden appearance in film of a photographed image.

Language is important. Likening the appearance of a spiritual image to a *process of precipitation*, emphasizes the condensation and intensification of physical particles into a cloud-like figure. Recalling Freud and Breuer's Studies on Hysteria, which laid the ground for Freud's understanding of traumatic repetition, the patient Anna O. (a pseudonym) described her somnambulant states or *condition-seconde* as "clouds" – implicitly grasping her own trance-like states as *condensations*, a word Freud would use again and again to name the affects and images that built-up within the patient throughout the day. These clouds of affective excess, the traumatic return of intensive quasi-autonomous atmospheres, would then *precipitate* to form bodily symptoms evident in the hysteric's contracted gestures and hallucinatory states. The precipitated symptom, as I understand it, is an effect of what was condensed or intensified in the body of the hysteric – affecting material of the past that is, by definition, always out-of-joint with the present. There is something continuous, beyond their shared 19th century modernity, between the figure of the hysteric and that of the Spiritualist medium; I see the hysteric as a figure that makes visible a transitional, sensory and spiritual body – a body frozen in mysterious gestures, chrysalis-like, tensed between actual and the virtual, past and future. A body formed through the condensation of entire 'atmospheres' of the past, articulated in physical gestures and a theater of inner images. These pasts return not as memories but as presences far more animate – what has not been laid to rest. The hysteric, conceived here as a transitional body, perhaps materializes what Deleuze has called the *body without organs*: the body that escapes the anatomical organization of the fleshly body. It is composed of thresholds of sensory intensity, arising out of yet irreducible to the material body, insofar as it composes an other 'sense' – one that escapes the organ-ization of the body.

In the case of 19th century hysteria, it is as if this second-body belongs to an elsewhere, made visible through the present aberrant physical states and somnambulant absences of the actual body. And not unlike the medium emerging from trance-states, the hysteric is marked by a forgetting of what happened in her "clouds," or *condition-seconde*. Breuer describes her inability to recognize people who were once familiar to her. In order to identity those around her, Anna O. had to run through an almost forensic list of singular attributes, one by one (presumably by touch), saying, "the nose is like this, and the hair like that, so it has to be so and so" (Freud & Breuer, 2004, p. 36). Anna O. is estranged by, but also performs an estrangement of, the anatomical order of the body, as much as the orders of recognition that govern the use of everyday language. Words become detached from their ordinary usage, a list of attributes isolated from recognizable context. The once familiar – the room, the family, the body itself – become unfamiliar. In a similar way, the medium, in sensing the inner presence of a spirit, must find a language to "paint" the unfamiliar realm of the dead, back to life, converting the *unheimlich* to the *heimlich*, so that a 'sitter' might recognize and receive this communication from the spirits.

The hysteric *precipitates the symptom*, materializing the affects of her somnambulant states in bodily pains, gestures, or by activating inner images as outer atmospheres, pasts you can move through in the present. Spirit painting, as a process of mediation, seems to *precipitates* both what lies in the inner space of the sitter and an animate presence, or the coincidence of these – of memory and spiritual presence; all this, through the body of the medium who is third-term in this transference. I borrow the term *conversion* from conversion-disorder (a more contemporary term for hysteria) here to name the transition whereby an inner, felt image of the dead becomes externalized in and through the energy of the medium, into yet another media – paint. In connecting such mediumistic *conversions* to the etiology of hysteria, my aim is not to reduce mediumship to hysteria or hysteria to mediumship, but to ask what lies between them, what is this shared spectral process whereby sensory images and atmospheres (affects) are converted to physical symptoms, or materialized as communicable figures for others? And what lurks here is also problem of history, namely of the failure of history: for mediumship makes visible a gap, a spectral space opened by the failure of such conversions. *Conversion disorder* here becomes a way of naming *the failure or gap opened by what cannot be converted to history*, and thus laid to rest. It is the bone in the throat, the affect – as word or image – that sticks in the body as symptom. The spirit returns, not as something already laid to rest – a person remembered – but as an animate spirit, persistent bone in the throat of the living.

During acts of precipitated painting, Nagy seems to consider the actual room itself to be transformed into a "fine dust," condensed and the precipitated upon the image that appears on the canvas. Nagy writes:

> The pot of multicolored paint [...] reacts to the combined magnetism of the mediums along with everything else in the room or space that is being used for the precipitation séance. The walls, rugs, curtains, and even flowers (which were often used) react to the magnetism and transform into the fine dust-like substance that creates the painting.

Of the material that appears on the canvas it is said to be "like soot" and "comes off on the finger, a smutty oil substance," and while somehow the paint pots are used during the precipitation of the image, Nagy says the portraits are not made of "paint, ink, pastel, nor *any known* substance [emphasis added]" (2010, p. 11). He adds, quoting a famous description of unknown origin, "it could be compared to the dust on a butterfly's wings," and wonders if this has something to do with the transformation of oil paint when "chemically altered by spirit" becoming "as light as pollen" and appearing as "spectrum-colored dust" (2010, p. 84).

What is this magical transition whereby space itself is precipitated into an image? The entire atmosphere, the room itself, by a strange material inversion, is condensed into image, an image *made of the space* become colorful dust, dust "as light as pollen" on the canvas. And if all paint pigments originate in nature before their modern chemical transubstantiation, what to make of this poetic transubstantiation of the present atmosphere into color – a spectrum of colors coloring the flesh of the spirit on canvas? The room thus condensed becomes a face, or maybe the substance through which a face can be *pressed* and take form. I can think of no better parallel to describe what occurs in mediumistic practice – where the outside (the spirits), become ephemeral sensations, an immaterial 'dust,' that passes through the surface of a body. The medium makes of her body an inner cabinet where, not only spirit-images, but entire spiritual atmospheres are precipitated as inner, dusty, foggy films.

As the only known precipitators of spirit paintings, according to Nagy, the Bang Sisters and Campbell Brothers are themselves legendary figures of physical mediumship. The paintings are impressive portraits in their own right – there is something slightly out of focus about them, something ethereal in the faces, particularly in those I've seen by the Bang Sisters. Two of the "finest" portraits by the Campbell Brothers hang in the Maplewood hotel at Lily Dale, in a modest sitting room just off of the front porch: an almost life-sized portrait of Azur the Great, the "guide" of the Campbell Brothers, and one of President Lincoln. As the historian Robert Cox notes, "according to opponents and proponents of the movement, even the White House was infested with Spiritualists." It is considered common knowledge among Spiritualists that Mary Todd Lincoln was a medium, and that séances were held at the White House.

There are many paintings by the Bang Sisters at Lily Dale, including a very ethereal portrait of a girl with golden hair, which hangs in the National Spiritualist Association of Churches office (NSAC) at Lily Dale, and a few others of what looks like idyllic stereotypes of "noble Indian" children, one entitled "Smart Weed" and the other "Blossom." The one of Blossom is of a Pocahontas-like figure wearing a white flowing costume and standing before Arcadian ruins and forest, as if in in a painting by Poussin. Exceeding the scope of this essay, I argue elsewhere that Spiritualism, as a mostly white, Anglo-American movement, is in complex (and obvious ways) shaped by settler colonial inheritances and imaginaries – most clearly found in the 19th century practice of channeling "Indian" spirits at the séance table, resonant with the broader American literary preoccupation with spectral or "ghostly" Indians.[2]

The following is an account describing the work of the Bang Sisters, Elizabeth S. and May E. Bangs of Chicago, "who had the gift of direct writing, drawing, and painting," but were most known for the richness of color and detail.

> Two identical [blank] paper mounted canvases in wooden frames were held up face to face against the window with the lower half resting upon a table, and the sides held by each sister with one hand. A short curtain was hung on either side, and an opaque blind was drawn over the canvases. The light streamed from behind the canvases, which were translucent, and after a quarter of an hour the outline of shadows began to appear and disappear as the invisible artist made a preliminary sketch; then the picture began to grow at a feverish rate. When the pictures were separated, the portrait was found on the surface of the canvas next to the "sitter."
> (Swann, 1897, p. 3)

The agency of sunlight is foregrounded here, light streaming through the window develops the spirit image, while the surface of the painting remains hidden behind a curtain. May Bangs wrote, in a letter of 1910, that "the room is shaded sufficiently to cause all the light from the window to pass through the canvas, thus enabling the sitter to witness the development and detect the least change in the shadows" (Nagy, 2010, pp. 10–11). It is as if the Bang sisters, credited with "the first recorded demonstration of precipitated spirit painting" in 1894, are mimicking the simple function of the camera, enclosing the canvas with dark curtains on all sides, and allowing light to stream in from a focal point. Nagy notes that in a later stage of their mediumistic "development," the Bang sisters no longer had need of this quasi-photographic apparatus, the "locked cabinet or curtained-off space," a process that sometimes took several "sittings" to complete – and "were openly precipitated, as if by airbrush, and some took as little as five minutes to complete" (2010, p. 82).

Also of note is the temporality of this image – the process is initially described as slow, then picking up speed "feverishly," until the portrait is completed, sometime in half an hour. "Much faster," as Nagy is fond of pointing out, than if it had been painted by human hands. In organizing the body, the paint, the canvas, and natural light in mimicry of photographic processes, such "demonstrations" of the working of spirit revealed the power of the body (spiritually, energetically, sensorially) as a superior technology – for the body can mediate not only images, but spirits. This also points to a deeper tension within Spiritualism; while the fact of bodily mediation is acknowledged in the very term – the Medium – it is simultaneously denied, insofar as the image must 'precipitate' without the artistic mediation of human hand or eye.

What is more, the images produced are not the statically dead images of the photograph as index of momentary reality, but animate images that respond and change, that is, behave in relation to the sitter and the medium. Even when the spirit image is materialized upon something as concrete as a canvas, the images *behave* like the images experienced in the inner theater of the Medium – that is, as a *dynamic image*. Often when the image appears, it will correct itself:

> The spirit entity that has now appeared and embedded his or her image on canvas may have a crooked bow tie or a hair out of place. The defect will disappear as if some motherly entity is mentally focusing on creating a perfect likeness.

Nagy notes repeatedly that the eyes will often "gradually open, giving a life-like appearance to the whole face" (2010, p. 11).

Stranger still, the image is responsive to the desires of the sitter – not unlike a witness describing a criminal to a forensic artist, the sitter may intervene in the paintings. Reportedly, a Mrs. Gertrude Breslan Hunt, from Norwood Park Illinois, requested a spirit painting by the famous Bang Sisters in 1909, but while the painting was "in process" she requested changes be made to the painting:

> Mrs. Hunt objected to the pose and asked that it be full face. The entire face obediently faced away and was rapidly re-sketched. Mrs. Hunt then commented that the hair was too light and the cheeks should be more colorful. As she sat observing, the shadows began to intensify in the waves of the hair until it darkened, the cheeks gained more color and the sleeves of the robe were also altered. (Nagy, 2010, p. 13)

What to make of these collaborative portraits, that animate, slowly opening their eyes to look back at the living, as they change to conform to the sitters' *memory* of their deceased loved one? If they are condensations of the energy and material of the room – into some particulate "unknown" matter, as Nagy says – they are also precipitations of the mnemonic images of the deceased we carry in us – as the intervention of the sitter upon the portrait shows. And yet, attributed an animate movement, these paintings are not images of *memories*, if by memory we mean something safely sequestered to a dead past.

It is interesting how images of the dead, so popular in the 19th century – memento mori of all kinds, including the death-mask and the spirit photograph – seem to engage a fated need, of how to make the past endure in the image, to insist beyond the death of the body. As if it is to the disappearance of the body that such images address themselves.

Maybe this is why there is an insistence in Nagy's accounts, echoing Spiritualist editorials, that spirit paintings are not "copies" of photographs. The portraits, says Nagy, do not "resemble" the photograph because they often differ in stance and apparel. Even when the sitter was invited to bring a photograph of the deceased with them, Nagy insists they did not show the medium the photograph but kept it concealed, until the portrait was finished. This emphasis on the medium having not seen the photograph seems to be a reassurance against the accusation that the medium is somehow copying the image – either directly from a photograph, or perhaps from her own memory onto the canvas – problematic, as such representational agency on the part of the medium, discounts the agency of spirits.

At the same time, an excerpt from the Spiritualist newspaper *The Sunflower* dated 1905, states that a Mr. & Mrs. Beckwith, who wanted portraits of the deceased children, "compared their portraits to the photographs [they had brought with them] and marveled at the likeness" (Nagy, 2010, p. 29). Nagy goes on to say that these portraits, apart from their being in color, "in all respects resemble photographs taken by a camera" (2010, p. 27). The verifiability of the spirit painting seems to depend on its *not* being merely *a copy* of an image – presumably to ward off the accusation that the Medium somehow copied the photograph – and yet, the fact that there should be a *resemblance* between the photograph (later revealed) and the painting, grounds the veracity of the spirit image. And given the distinction drawn here between true image and copy, what of the set-up used by the Bang sisters that, in its initial phases, resembles *a photographic experiment* – the canvas curtained off like a black-box, light streaming in from a single location? Why, in other words, the emphasis on painting as a spiritual medium, instead of photography, since photography is the emergent technology of the mid-19th century, and is mimicked in the very operation of spirit painting? Especially, within a tradition that spiritualizes photography by inventing spirit photography? The distinction between photographs and paintings, analogous to that between memory and spirit presence, seems aimed at securing the image as animate and *auratic*, that is, original in some sense. Yet the analogy to photography figures the medium as a reproductive technology: one who can reproduce the "image" again and again, albeit differentially, with the help of the spirits. Yet the claim here is that spirit painting betrays a strange liveliness and plasticity in the image that a static photograph, index of a sudden exposure, cannot: the look of life in the eyes, the accommodating shifts and changes after exposure. Recall the eyes, which are said to open after the séance as the painting changes and conforms to the will of the sitter, "as if some motherly entity is mentally focusing on creating a perfect likeness" (Nagy, 2010, p. 3). The emphasis is not on the painted image as "perfect likeness" but as a living and dynamic entity – thus an animate and changing entity – like the portrait of Dorian Gray, only instead of revealing the dark-side, the spirit is *always* portrayed at their best, in a spiritual light.

A distinction between spirit photography and precipitated painting also lies in the role of the medium. When precipitating a painting, the Medium is engaging with the spirits actively and energetically, while, by contrast, spirit photographs are treated as second-order indexical evidence of the *event* of spirit presence. Spirit photographs, as an indexical record, are understood as evidential images of an always prior *event* of mediumistic spirit materialization, and not, as in the precipitated spirit image, of an animate, changing spirit figure congealed in paint.

Thus the mechanical set-up of spirit painting mimicking the photographic apparatus so as to emphasize the lack of human intervention in the process – consistent with what has been called the "ideology of mechanical objectivity" – at once directs us away from human agency while claiming an other-than-human agency, the agency of the spirit (Daston & Galison 2007). The Medium thus imitates the photographic apparatus, while claiming to do with her body what the photograph cannot do – that is, to see and sense what the "objective" camera eye, or the naked eye for that matter, cannot see – what is, at least visibly and visually, *not there*. For the image precipitated is, after all, of the dead.

The sense I draw from all this is that somehow spirit painting, in directing images back through the body, directs us toward the mystery of bodily mediation: the body as a *medium of all media* and the condition of the re-animation of not only "dead" spirits, but "dead" (as in reproducible) images (Wegenstein, 2020).

For if spirit painting congeals the atmosphere of the present – the actual room in which the painting process is taking place – it also enfolds this present atmosphere with what is *absent*, and seemingly incommunicable, the dead. The remembered images, as held in the past-tense of the indexical photograph – this happened! – as well as the absent-dead who are by definition in *the past*—are thereby re-animated by mixing with the stuff, the subtle affective "dust," of the *the present* atmosphere.

We can still see the residual emphasis on painting, despite a decline in such practices, in the very common language Mediums today use to describe spirit communication as "painting the dead back to life." Perhaps painting, more so than photography, is a chosen medium of the spirits because painting and mediumship share a zone of indiscernibility: they both turn the body inside-out, as a media of extension sensorially reaching out to capture atmospheres and ephemeral images, only to congeal these, in a second moment, in the materiality of color and paint. And yet, unlike most approaches to painting, there is this insistent lack of the trace of the hand (in the gestures of mark making) in precipitated painting that hides the mediation of the body.

Spirit painting seems to confuse inside and outside, image and space, *externalizing* an immaterial sensory event occurring *within* the medium, while materially *condensing* space itself, pulverized into a paint-like sensory dust. Space – all that may be called atmosphere – is said to be condensed in the making of this two-dimensional image. In this sense, painting points us toward the temporality of visionary experience itself, not only as an imagistic event within the body, but as a spatial unfolding of animate atmospheres: inner "theaters" (recalling the hysteric) of sensation communicated through hand, eye and color, releasing "presences beneath representation, beyond representation" (Deleuze 2003, 45). The spirit, through the mediating body, makes itself visible – here manifest on canvas and in color – as a living-after-effect of the embodied vision that occurs *before*, in the body of the medium. Or there is a collapsing of *before* and *after*, the visionary experience of the body and the manifestation of the spirit in paint, in a simultaneous moment.

Notes

1 Though often discreetly practiced, during my fieldwork I heard practitioners speculate that physical mediumship was again 'on the rise.'
2 See Yerby (2017), Berland (2000), and Cox (2003).

References

Bergland, R. (2000). *The national uncanny: Indian ghosts and American subjects*. University Press of New England.
Cox, R. S. (2003). *Body and soul: A sympathetic history of American spiritualism*. University of Virginia Press.
Daston, L., & Gallison, P. (2007). *Objectivity*. Zone Books.
Deleuze, G. (2003). *Francis Bacon: The logic of sensation* (D. W. Smith, Trans.). University of Minnesota Press.
Freud, S., & Breuer, J. (2004). *Studies in hysteria* (N. Luckhurst, Trans.). Penguin Books.
Kandinsky, W. (1977). *Concerning the spiritual in art* (M. T. H. Sadler, Trans.). Dover Publications.

Nagy, R. (2010). *Precipitated painting*. Galde Press.

Swann, I. (1897). The Bangs Sisters and their precipitated spirit portraits. In *Light of truth album*. The Light of Truth Publishing Company.

Wegenstein, B. (2020). Body. In W. J. T. Mitchell & M. B. N. Hansen (Eds.), *Critical terms for media studies* (pp. 19–34). University of Chicago Press.

Yerby, E. (2017). *Spectral bodies of evidence: The body as medium in American spiritualism*. ProQuest LLC.